SUMMER SIZZLERS & MAGIC MONDAYS:

School-Age Theme Activities

By Edna Wallace

FREE After School Resource Catalog

School-Age NOTES

P.O. Box 40205
Nashville, TN 37204
1-800-410-8780
www.AfterSchoolCatalog.com

Published By School-Age Notes
P.O. Box 40205 • Nashville, Tennessee 37204

ABOUT THE AUTHOR

Edna Wallace has taught preschool, owned and directed child care centers and now works as a consultant specializing in staff and curriculum development.

She has conducted workshops at the state and national level and supports families though parent education.

She is editor and publisher of the Parent Pages Newsletter.

Computer Graphic Layout By: Diane Neel

Library of Congress Catalog Card Number: 94-69466
ISBN: 0-917505-06-9

10 9 8 7 6 5 4 3

© Copyright 1994. **Pages, Inc.**
All Rights Reserved.
Published by **School-Age** NOTES P.O. Box 40205, Nashville, TN 37204

"Printed on 50% recycled paper. For every 1000 copies of this book, 5 mature trees have been saved."

DEDICATION

*This Book is dedicated
to my husband,
Richard Wallace,
for being a true ally
in this endeavor.*

*To my children,
Brent, Kelly ,
and Ann Marie
for adding magic to ordinary days.*

*And to all the children at
Little Folks
Discovery Center
who included me
in their world of play and learning.*

INTRODUCTION

SUMMER SIZZLERS & MAGIC MONDAYS: **School-Age Theme Activities** offers you new theme ideas and activities for summer and after school programs. In a unique format, the book is divided into two sections;

SUMMER SIZZLERS, with themes designed to emphasize summer day activities -
MAGIC MONDAYS, with activities suitable for the hours after school.

School-age children spend a great deal of time laboring with paper and pencils, struggling with acceptable social behavior, and in general conforming to adult standards. While these tasks are necessary for social and intellectual growth, it's also critical to provide experiences which delight, inspire, and capture the spirit of children.

This book is a written extension of many hours spent with children as explorers on summer days and during their time after school. It's for adults with a passion for creating playful, enriching environments for children and for adults who remember what it was like to be a child - what it was like to start clubs, collect things, run through sprinklers, and feed ants.

At this age children are intensely aware of similarities and differences between genders, cultures and races. It's an ideal time to focus on opportunities that allow for an appreciation of diversity. Care has been taken to include activities that help children respect individual differences.

SUMMER SIZZLERS AND MAGIC MONDAYS expand upon daily experiences with ideas that draw upon the rich imagination of children and their limitless capability to have fun. Each theme may be expanded upon to create interest that lasts a day or a lifetime. When children are included in the planning, summer and after school programs are guaranteed to be lively and powerful experiences!

SUMMER SIZZLERS

TABLE OF CONTENTS

MAGIC MONDAYS

SUMMER

SIZZLERS

Bagels are delicious, but they're good for lots of other things too.

Try playing these games and activities for some fun-filled days.

BAGEL BASH

Bagel Beginnings

What's a bagel? A bagel is a hard yeast roll twisted into a doughnut shape. It is then cooked in simmering water and baked. Yummy!

Make A Word

How many three letter words can you make from BAGEL?
How about, bag, leg, gal, lag, beg, gab

Bite The Bagel!

Play this game for lots of fun and good nutrition too! Tie a string around each bagel and hang it from a tree or piece of playground equipment. Make sure it hangs down to mouth level.

At the word "GO," each player (with their hands behind their backs) tries to "bite the bagel." It's pretty tricky because the bagel moves every time it is touched, so ...

OPEN WIDE! When the game is over, serve some bagels with cream cheese.

Tongue Twisters

Baby Betsy Bites Bagels
Ben Bought Billions of Baskets of Bagels

Beaded Bagel

Cut bagels in half. Spread with cream cheese or another favorite topping. Give each school-ager an assortment of raisins, snips of marshmallows and M&M's. See who can "bead" the bagel in the most creative way. Choose the winners in these categories:

Best Bagel *(Best all-around)*

Beautiful Bagel *(The most attractive)*

Better Bagel *(Most creative)*

Blimp Bagel *(Most fattening)*

Bagel Bag

Stale bagels are great for print art with bright, beautiful colors . Decorate a brown paper grocery bag for keeping neat stuff in.

Put tempera paint in shallow styrofoam meat trays. Cut the bagels into different shapes—triangles, stars, hearts etc.

The children can dip the bagels into the paint and make prints on the bag. The bags may also be folded around books to make great book covers.

Sand Castles

Mix water with sand in the sandbox . Provide styrofoam cups and various empty tin cans of all sizes.

Pack the wet sand into the cans and turn them over for fabulous turrets. Set a time limit and give a prize for the most fabulous castle.

Play "Surfin' Safari"

Place a sheet on the ground to represent the ocean. Put on some surfing music—how about "Surfin' Safari" by the Beach Boys?

While the music plays, the school-agers "surf" back and forth across the ocean. But when the music stops, the surfers are caught unless they are back on the beach.

Surfers must move continuously back and forth across the ocean; they can't always stay close to the beach. The surfers that are caught have to stay on the beach. Whoever "surfs" the longest wins the game.

Beach Bubbles

Make a home-made batch of bubbles by mixing these ingredients. Make a bubble blower by bending a coat hanger into a circle. Wow, giant beach bubbles!

1	quart water
8	tbsp. liquid detergent
4	tbsp. glycerin
2	tsp. sugar

What's more fun in the summer than going to the beach—sunning, swimming, and searching for shells? Create a relaxing beach atmosphere inside.

Ask the children to bring their suits, towels and sunblock. Don't forget imaginations!

Beach Riddle # 1

How do you say goobye to a sand castle?
With a wave!

Beach Riddle # 2

What did the beach say as the tide came in ?
"Long time no sea."

Beach Bats

It's lots of fun to play games on the beach.
Make beach bats from wire coat hangers and
panty hose. Shape the coat hanger into a
large circle and then stretch a section of
panty hose over it.

The hook of the hanger becomes the handle.
School-agers can bat foam balls or balls made
from wadded up newspaper or tinfoil back and forth.

Sand Paintings

Place sand in medium sized margarine containers.
Mix a few tablespoons of tempera paint with the sand.
Give each child a baby food jar and a spoon.
Let them spoon the colored sand into layers
inside the jar. The sand should come to the
top of the jar. When the painting is finished,
place a piece of cotton on top before putting
the lid on. This will keep the sand from shifting
when the jar is moved. For a finishing touch,
cover the lid with aluminum foil or
paint it with tempera paint.

Beach Mural

Make a BEACH MURAL that will cover an entire wall. Measure butcher paper at least 6 feet long—cut two pieces. One piece will become the sandy beach and the other the ocean and sky. When the mural is finished it will be taped together at the back for a beautiful beach scene.

Have one half of the class work on the beach and the other half work on the ocean.

MAKE THE SCENE REALISTIC BY USING REAL MATERIALS WHEN POSSIBLE:

Sandy Beach

Spread glue evenly over the paper and sprinkle sand on top. Pat the sand down so that it will stay on the paper. If at all possible, glue real shells onto the sand. For palm trees glue on some real bark and some fern leaves.

Ocean And Sky

Water paint the ocean with blue and green watercolors. Use cottonballs for clouds. Children can cut seagulls and fish from construction paper. Now, relax on beach towels with a cool glass of lemonade, and dream of sunning on the beach!

Play Beach Blanket Bum

Place school-agers' towels on the ground side by side.
Have one less towel than the number of children!

Have the players line up behind a marker.
At the word "GO" they race to lay on a towel.
Only one person per towel, please!

At each turn, remove one towel.
The last person to be laying on a towel
is the real "Beach Blanket Bum!"

FISHNET PICTURE

Have the school-agers color
a styrofoam meat tray with blue
markers or colors.
Glue real shells and paper fish,
seaweed etc. inside the tray.

Cover the tray with a small piece of fishnet or vegetable
bag netting, taping at back. Something's fishy about this picture!

Hide And Go Shell

Before the beach party begins,
hide some shells in the sandbox.

Give each school-ager a shovel and pail.
At the word "GO" let them
start digging for shells.

CREATE A COMMERCIAL

Forget- Me - Not Names

Names of products are very important. Give your school-agers a chance to dream up some names for these new products: shampoo, soap, chewing gum, breakfast cereal, gym shoes, etc.

EXAMPLES:

BATCH OF BUBBLES
CAPTAIN CLEAN   GOOFY GUM
YUMMY CRISPS   MIGHTY SNEAKERS

To extend the activity, ask everyone to make lists of as many products as they can such as Pepsi, Crayola, Kleenex, Life-Savers, Snickers, Salon Selectives, etc. Give them five minutes to compile lists, then compare!

Design A Bottle

Use the pattern on page 127. Ask your school-agers to design a bottle or jar around the label. Tell them to use their imaginations - jars and bottles come in all shapes and sizes!

Create A Commercial

That was pretty easy!
Now the assignment is to create a commercial.
Before beginning this activity talk about why people buy things. Have everyone think of a commercial they think is particularly clever. Have them think of a commercial they can't get out of their heads.
What makes a commercial hard to forget?

After the discussion ask the children to make up a television commercial for a new type of dog food, tooth paste, or paper towel. Once they've dreamed up a new product, they can write a script for the commercial.

The next step is to choose some simple props and the actors. Now comes the fun part—each group gets to practice the commercial and act it out in front of the class.

Commercials are advertising campaigns that try to sell things. School-agers probably see many commercials on TV every day that make them want to buy a certain toy, a candy bar, shoes, etc. This fun activity gives them the opportunity to create their own advertisement.

Awards For Winners!

At the end of this activity, give commercial awards like:

Funniest, Most Original, BEST ALL-AROUND!

To make this activity less competitive and more effort-oriented,
find something special about each pencil holder.

Commercials Aren't Always Fair!

To raise awareness about cultural diversity, ask school-agers to view commercials with a critical eye. Ask school-agers to ponder these questions:

Can you think of a commercial where women are treated as silly or stupid?

Can you think of a commercial that includes a person with limited physical abilities?

Can you think of a commercial that shows a different type of family or a minority race?

As a class, make up a commercial or change a commercial to make it fair!

Recycled Labels

Labels are colorful and appealing in many ways.
Ask children to bring in some labels from products such as shampoo and food. Next, let them cover an empty juice can with glue and stick the labels on.
When finished, these make great pencil holders.

Cooking is an activity that most children thoroughly enjoy. Sampling the food is even more fun!
The following recipes are easy and nutritious!

Camper's Mix

2   qts. popped corn
1   cup peanuts
1   cup raisins
1   cup flaked coconut
1   cup sunflower seeds

Mix ingredients well and season with a litte salt if desired.
Store in an airtight container.
This is a great mix to take on a hike!

No-Bake Cookies

5   tbsp. cocoa
1/2 cup evaporated milk
1   tsp. vanilla
2   cups sugar
1   stick margarine
3   cups rolled oats
1/2 cup chopped nuts

Mix cocoa, milk, vanilla, sugar and margarine in saucepan,
boil for 1 minute. Add oats and nuts. Drop onto waxed paper by teaspoons and cool.
NO BAKING!

MULTICULTURAL COOKING

A great way to learn about different cultures is by sampling their food. These recipes are especially welcome because they are easy and sure to become favorites.

Quesadilla

8	flour tortillas
2	cups cooked chicken *(diced)*
1/8	cup diced cilantro
1/4	tsp. cumin
1/2	tsp. salt
1	tsp. pepper
3	cups shredded cheddar

Lightly butter one side of tortillas, place on sheet pan butter side up. Set pan to the side. Mix cumin, salt, pepper and cilantro together with the chicken. Spread the mixture on tortillas, top with cheese.

Bake at 350° for 4-8 minutes.

• *Cilantro is an herb similar to parsley and may be found in most stores in the produce department.*

Jicama *(Mexican potato pronounced heekama)*

Jicama is in the tuber family. Its large roots contain a crisp, white center that has a pleasant, sweet taste.

Peel 3-4 roots and slice into 1/4th inch strips and eat raw.

Jicama can be found in most produce departments.

(English) **Apple-Sauce**

2 1/2 pounds peeled and wedged apples
2/3   cup sugar
2   tbsp. cinnamon
8   oz. apple juice

In large pot heat apples until they start to brown.
Add apple juice, sugar and cinnamon.
Continue stirring until apple wedges cook into small pieces.

Serve hot.

Teriyaki Sauce

4   cups soy sauce
2/3   cup brown sugar
2 1/4 tbsp. crushed garlic
1/2   tbsp. fresh ginger (fine diced)
1/4   cup onion (fine diced)
1/2   tsp. salt

Sauté garlic, onions and ginger in butter until the onions
are translucent. Add the soy sauce and brown sugar.
Bring to a boil. Reduce heat and simmer for 10 minutes.
Salt and pepper to taste. Thicken with cornstarch if desired.

Great for dipping fish and vegetables!

Recipes For Fun

Peanut Butter Playdough

peanut butter
honey
powdered milk

Remind school-agers to wash their hands!
Mix equal amounts of peanut butter, honey and powdered milk in a small bowl.
After stirring together, mix with hands until dough forms.
Let children use the dough for sculpting and eat it when they're done!

Apple Chip Cones

Pour apple sauce in ice trays. When frozen, remove from trays and
crush in a blender or place in plastic bag and crush with a kitchen mallet.
Spoon apple chips into ice cream cones for a refreshing snack.

Riddle Roundup

**Why was the woman surprised
when an apple fell on her head?**

Because she was sitting under a peach tree!

Collecting is FUN! This is a project that can be added to over time. It's more rewarding to begin at the start of your summer program so the children can help each other with their collections. It provides a great sense of accomplishment to reach goals and display collections for others to admire.

Parent Involvement

Let parents know what the children are collecting so they have an opportunity to send in items that might be needed.

Have A Peek-In

At the end of summer, display the various collections. Serve some simple refreshments and let the parents have an opportunity to observe what the children have been involved in.

What To Collect?

People enjoy collecting all sorts of things. Some collections are worth lots of money, others are purely for enjoyment. If you or someone you know has a collection, bring it in and share it with the kids.

On the following pages are suggestions appropriate for this age group.

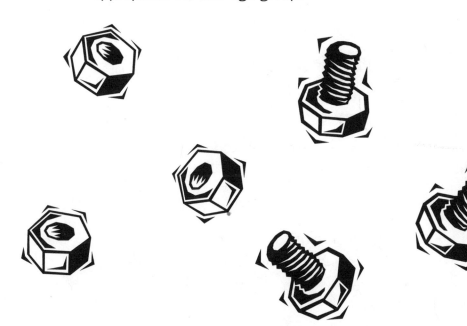

BOTTLE CAPS

Collect bottle caps from soda bottles and
all sorts of food items from ketchup to syrup.
Think of all the cleaning supplies that have
interesting caps like Windex and Fantastic.
Another group is shampoo, lotion etc.
WOW—The possibilities seem endless!

DISPLAY: *Shoeboxes, Berry Boxes or Egg Cartons*

Business Cards

This collection can be started with business cards
from friends and family. Business cards arrive in the
mail with advertising and brochures. Almost every
professional has a business card and sometimes
they are on display in stores.

They can be arranged according to color of card,
location of business or type of business.

DISPLAY: *Shoeboxes or Scrapbook*

Matchbook Covers

**THIS IS A COLLECTION OF COVERS ONLY:
REMOVE MATCHES.**

Lots of businesses, especially restaurants, give out matches.
This can be a very colorful and interesting collection.

DISPLAY:

*Glue onto sheets of paper.
Hang from string stretched across a wall or
bulletin board.*

Gum Wrappers

What a great idea for recycling those little bits of paper that would otherwise be thrown outl

DISPLAY:

Smooth them out and stack in groups of 10.
Mold them into a ball and see how big the ball grows.
Fold them into lengths and make into a chain.

Buttons

Just about everybody has buttons around the house.
Collect different shapes and sizes, different colors, plain or fancy.
Once again, the possibilities are almost endless!

DISPLAY: *Egg Cartons or Small Boxes*

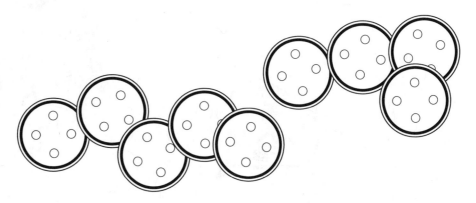

Postcards

Postcards old and new are beautiful to look at.
The kids can collect them on vacations and get
them from stores, friends and relatives.
Some categories for collecting postcards might be:

cities, animals, buildings, parks, nature scenes, etc.

DISPLAY: *Shoeboxes, Scrapbooks, Bulletin board*

Stamps

This is one of the most popular collections.
Everyone gets stamps on letters almost everyday.
It's amazing how many varieties there are.
These can be categorized according to dates
issued, cost, pictures of people, animals,
countries, etc.
Collections may be bought or
collected from families and friends.

DISPLAY: *Stamp albums with clear pockets on the page are popular.
Corners and hinges are also available for mounting in
notebooks and scrapbooks.*

Dads are very special people and the school-agers will have a chance to show how much they care with these gifts and activities.

COUPON BOOK

Busy fathers appreciate help around the house and yard. One of the most thoughtful gifts a child can give is a COUPON BOOK filled with jobs they can do for their dads.

Encourage children to think up jobs their father would truly appreciate:

WALK THE DOG	MAKE THE BED
WASH THE CAR	BACK RUB
BREAKFAST IN BED	FOLD CLOTHES
VACUUM CARPET	RUN BATH WATER

Use the coupon pattern on page 131.
Cut out the coupons, write personal messages on them and staple together to make a coupon book.

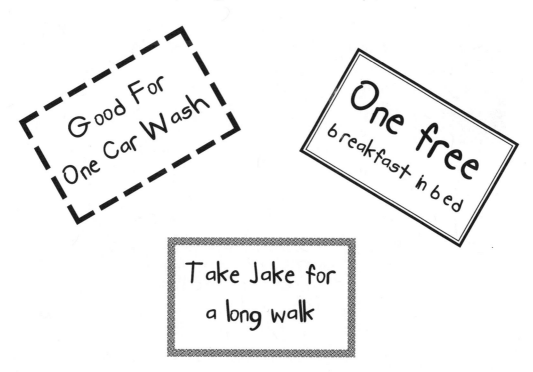

Pretty Pots

Collect small plastic flower pots.
Have each child bring one from home or
see if a local nursery will donate them
to your program.

Cut jute into 12 to 15 inch lengths. Next, spread glue evenly over the bottom half of the pot. Start wrapping the jute from the bottom of the pot to where glue ends. Cover the rest of the pot with glue and continue to wrap with jute until the pot is completely covered. Working with half of the pot at one time keeps the glue from drying out.

Dads appreciate flowers too. Plant a pretty flower in the pretty pot.

Money Bowl

Make a money bowl for your dad's loose change!

Mix up a batch of modeling clay, then mold it into a small bowl. Before it dries, press some pennies into the clay. It will take about one day to dry.

Modeling Clay

Mix 2 cups flour and 1 cup of salt in a small bowl.
Gradually add 1/2 cup of water until mixture forms
soft modeling clay.

Bookmark

Cut construction paper in strips
two inches wide by eight inches long.

Completely cover the bookmark on
one side with stickers or paper shapes.

SUGGESTIONS:

HEARTS *(To show love, love, love)*
SHAMROCKS *(For the Irish dads out there)*
ANIMALS *(For the animal lovers)*
POSTAGE STAMPS *(For the stamp collector)*

On the other side have children write
a personal Father's Day message.
Cover the bookmarks on both sides
with clear contact paper.

Celebrate Father's Day

Invite fathers to come by at the end of the day on the
Friday before Father's Day.

Serve simple refreshments like popcorn and lemonade.
The school-agers can give their gifts
and cards at this time.

*T*ake time to smell the roses.

Summer is the perfect time to do just that. Take field trips to botanical gardens, florists and nurseries. Often, these places will be happy to give you supplies of florists' wire, artificial flowers and maybe even some seeds to be used in "Flower Power" projects.

Create A Flower

Combine flower names to make up names for new flowers.

DAFFODIL	ROSE
PETUNIA	DAISY
MARIGOLD	TULIP
CARNATION	GLADIOLA

How about?   DALIP
ROTU
MARIROSE

Ask school-agers to draw a picture of their new flower.

Patsy picked pretty petals.
Flying flowers fluttered forever.

Pressed Petals

Select special flowers for pressing. Place the flowers between sheets of newspaper to soak up moisture from the flower. The paper will need to be changed several times before the flower is perfectly dry.

The next step is to tape the flower in place on a sheet of paper and cover it with cellophane.

Make a cover for the book from flowered wallpaper. Staple several sheets of pressed flowers together to make a scrapbook.

Sowing seeds

Give each child half of an egg carton.
Let them place dirt in the six empty egg cups.
Give them a few seeds from six different types of
flowers to plant in the different sections.
Cover the seeds with a little more dirt.

Place the egg cartons in a sunny window and
keep soil moist. The best way to moisten is by
spraying soil lighty with a spray bottle filled with water.
Pouring water directly on the seeds
tends to drown them!

Ask children to record
observations about the seeds:

which come up first?

what color are the seedlings?

when do they need transplanting?

which need more moisture, etc.?

Petal Pictures

Glue a real stem and real leaves onto
a sheet of construction paper.

Draw petals on and fill in the petals
with flower seeds to make a beautiful,
touchable picture.

Delightful Daisies

Your kids can make cheerful daisies
from balloons and pom-poms.
**(BE CAUTIOUS WHEN USING
UNINFLATED BALLOONS.
INSTRUCT CHILDREN NOT TO
PUT THEM IN THEIR MOUTHS.)**

Glue UNINFLATED white or yellow balloons into a circular daisy
pattern on a sheet of construction paper. Glue a pom-pom in
the center of the flower. Next, glue on a construction paper
stem, and glue green balloons on for the leaves.

This activity also works well for a class bulletin board project.
Instead of making individual pictures, glue balloon flowers
onto a construction paper flowerbox.

Seed Snack

Serve sunflower seeds for a snack. For a special treat,
sprinkle the seeds with a dash of soy sauce and
bake on a cookie sheet at low temperature for 5 minutes.
WARM, CRUNCHY AND DELICIOUS !

Make it a RED, WHITE AND BLUE DAY full of games and party treats.

School-agers are usually not in school on the Fourth of July, but that's no reason not to set aside a day to celebrate this very special birthday of the United States!

St★rs And Stripes Decorations

Decorate from floor to ceiling inside and out.
Start with the fence around the play ground.
Weave red, white and blue crepe paper through
a cyclone fence. Place streamers on the posts
to blow in the wind. An important thing to
remember is to remove the paper before
it starts to disintegrate and litters the landscape.

Cover cardboard stars with aluminum foil and
hang from the ceiling. Make banners and posters
to hang around the room. Hang strips of crepe paper in
different lengths from the doorway and drape it
from the ceiling.

Flag
Waving

Use the flag and stars pattern on page 135.
Copy a page for each child and let them dream up their own
ways of using them.

Happy Birthday

What's a birthday without a cake?
Mix up a cake mix and pour batter into
a 9 X 12 inch cake pan.
Bake the cake as directed and
then decorate like a flag using
candy red hots for stripes and
silver balls for stars. If that's a
little too sweet for your sweet tooth,
try the variation below.

Spread white frosting or cream cheese on the cake and decorate
with tiny American Flag toothpicks. These are available in party stores
and they're very inexpensive. Give a flag with each cake serving.
CAUTION THE CHILDREN AGAINST PLAYING WITH THE TOOTHPICKS.

FIREWORKS Picture

First, make a picture frame by cutting the center out of two sheets of
black construction paper, leaving one inch along all four sides on each sheet.

Sprinkle red, white and blue crayon shavings
onto waxed paper for patriotic fireworks.
Try orange, red and yellow shavings to represent
flames. Silver, white and gold make a spectacular
sparkling fireworks picture. Cover with a second
sheet of waxed paper. With a warm iron,
lightly press over the picture.
(AN ADULT MUST SUPERVISE THIS ACTIVITY.)

Spread glue on the edges of construction paper.
Mount the fireworks picture in between the
frames for a striking picture that looks
beautiful hanging in a window.

Star Spangled
Banner Picnic

Lunch is just more exciting when eaten outside.
Plan a picnic lunch with some special foods.

Put a few drops of red food coloring in softened cream cheese.
Spread between bread to make a sandwich.
Next, cut into a star shape with a star-shaped cookie cutter.

Take along some blue lemonade *(add a couple drops of blue food coloring)* and, of course, birthday cake or apple pie for dessert!

All American Birthday Present

Organize a litter patrol and see how many things can be collected that are recyclable.
Use the WANTED POSTER on page 141 to make the job easier.

If at all possible, plan a field trip to a recycling center and take some newspaper, glass, etc. in for recycling.

Recycle Ribbons

Use the ribbon pattern on page 139.

Explain that this symbol means a
product was made from materials
that can be or were recycled.
Reproduce these ribbons on paper
that has been used on one side,
and give one to each child.
They can wear the symbol proudly!

Encourage children to look for the
symbol on boxes, paper, grocery bags, etc.

Honest Abe

Everyone knows that Abraham Lincoln was an honest man.
Try this game for lots of laughs. Each child gets to make
3 statements about themselves. The catch is,
only one statement is really true.
The other children have to figure out
what 'Honest Abe' is lying about!

Examples

I have one brother and two sisters.
I like to play soccer.
I've been to Disneyland two times.

★'s & ●'s *(Stars & Dots)*

Make a patriotic flag from stars and stripes, or should we say
stars and dots! There are hundreds of signal dots and stars in
a single package or roll—
purchase them at any office supply store.

Have the school-agers draw a rectangle using a ruler.
Next, let them count the stripes on the flag and
draw these lines with the ruler. To make the red and white
stripes, they will need to stick the signal dots in a straight line.
Last, but not least, they will stick 50 stars on the flag.
This project takes lots of time, but they'll be proud
of the finished project.

Quite often children come to your summer program from different schools – even different states. The sooner they get to know each other the better! Try a few of these "ice-breakers" during the first few days.

Roll An Orange

Have school-agers stand in a line. Give the first person an orange. It must be held under the chin and then passed to the next person in line. That person must maneuver the orange under their chin, and pass it to the next person in line.

The trick here is hands can't be used at all! This game is really lots of laughs and it breaks down barriers in record time!

Select A Shoe

For this game, everyone must take off their shoes and pile them in the middle of the room. Be sure the shoes are all mixed up!

Next, form a circle around the shoes. At the word "GO" everyone rushes to the shoe pile and retrieves their own shoes. In order to win, the shoes have to be on, buckled and tied completely!

Reporter's Notebook

Cut scrap paper into pieces about 3 X 5 inches
and staple at the top to create a pad of paper.
Give a "notebook" and a pencil to each school-ager.

Ask them to interview other children in the
program and find out something about that
person they didn't know before.
As they get the "scoop," they
write down the facts in
their notebook.

The children may want to
spend another afternoon
reporting what they learned
to the rest in the program!

Personal Portrait

This exercise promotes an appreciation for diversity —
yet demonstrates we are alike in many ways.
Let children draw a name from a hat.
This will be their partner and
they will take turns drawing each other.
Ask children to look at each other
and ask these questions:

"What color are his eyes?
Does she wear glasses?
What color is his skin?
Is her hair straight or
curly, long or short?"

Children may exchange portraits
when they are finished.

Compliment Card

Frequently, children's strengths stand out to others in the class, and the compliment cards they collect give them a good idea of what their friends like about them.

Collecting "Warm Fuzzies" puts a nice glow on everyone's face and keeps children focused on the positive.

Cut small cards from tagboard. Give each school-ager a card for each child in the their group.
Ask them to finish the sentence:

"What I like most about you is.."

EXAMPLES:

smile, imagination, hair, friendly, sense of humor

Once this has been done, let them design a card for each person in their group. When the cards are completed, write the name of the child to receive the card on the back. The cards may be hand delivered by the sender until everyone has their collection of compliment cards. Another option is for the sender to remain anonymous. In this case, the teacher collects all of the cards and then delivers them to the right child.

*K*eeping a journal is a very rewarding experience. During the summer months, it's a fun way to keep up with language and writing skills. Hopefully the summer is planned with many field trips in mind and these will become highlights of the journal.

JAZZY JOURNAL

Keeping A Journal

This is a great habit for children to get into.
Encourage them to jot down, on a daily basis,
things that interest them. If they really don't want
to write, start them out with recording
the weather or the favorite
activity of the day.

Clever Covers

Have school-agers make
covers that show what
they are interested in.
Instead of using
construction paper,
try wallpaper in different
designs, sheet music,
personal art work, blueprints, fabric covered cardboard, etc.
Most decorators and architects are happy to give you their old
books or plans.

Staple several sheets of lined paper inside the covers—
make sure there are some blank sheets also for sketching.

Recording Field Trips

After each summer field trip,
set aside a few minutes for children
to record some of their favorite activities.
It's much easier to remember and
record activities that have just occurred.

If cameras are available,
let children take turns taking pictures.

My Favorites

Set aside a few pages for these special recordings:

FAVORITE SUMMER ACTIVITY
DESCRIBE YOUR TEACHER
DESCRIBE YOUR BEST SUMMER CAMP FRIEND
FAVORITE FIELD TRIP

Autograph PARTY

Have an autograph party! Sharpen the pencils, collect your pens, it's time for school-agers to sign their "John Henry."

Ask children to leave a few pages at the back of their "Jazzy Journals" for an autograph page.

Everyone, of course, must bring their journals to the party.

Encourage children to get autographs from staff, parents and other adults.

Names

Ask children to make up a new name for themselves.
Write the names on the board and encourage children
to call each other by the new names all day.
This activity takes lots of concentration even for the adult!

Make the whole day very mysterious from beginning to end. Be sure to read some mysteries to the children. This age benefits greatly from stories read aloud.

SPY
The Mystery Word

Use the pattern on page 143 for a fun word search game. Copy one for each child or laminate the page to use over and over again.

```
I  L  J  G  T  U  D  X  W  P  G
G  N  F  U  G  B  M  S  P  Y  H
S  Q  V  N  R  S  V  E  L  O  Z
A  W  K  E  Y  N  X  C  U  M  A
R  J  M  Y  S  T  E  R  Y  P  D
Q  X  A  F  H  T  G  E  L  O  L
S  K  G  T  B  R  I  T  D  W  G
F  N  I  A  K  T  R  G  E  K  V
S  J  C  L  U  E  S  F  A  Y  A
S  F  H  K  E  Y  I  P  S  T  D
G  R  W  N  G  U  Z  C  O  D  E
```

Fingerprints

For this activity you will need some good felt stamp pads. Show children how fingerprints are taken by rolling thumb from one side to another on a sheet of paper. This may take a bit of practice.

The bigger, the better. After getting a good fingerprint from each child, let the children look at them with a magnifying glass.

Fingerprint Match-up

Place a fingerprint of each child on a
small sheet of paper about the same size as
a playing card. Be sure and put the child's
name on the back of his or her print.
Have several magnifying glasses available.
When the fingerprints are completely dry,
mix them up and see if children can recognize
their own print.

Secret ⁜□❄❄▲ (Codes)

Make up some secret codes.

Try some clapping codes.

For example: two long claps and one short clap can mean
"Everyone be quiet," two long claps can mean "everyone sit down."

Make a certain word such as **"great"** really mean **"terrible."**

How about having a pass-word like **"flower"** mean **"yes."**
Everytime the school-agers hear the word flower,
they will know it really means **"yes."**

Ghost Writing

Write messages that disappear! Give school-agers a sheet of paper and
a Q-tip. Put a few bowls of lemon juice in the middle of the table.

Tell the kids to write their secret messages using the Q-tips dipped in lemon
juice. When dry, hold the paper over a light bulb to see what it says.

Nature Painting

Select some natural paint brushes and get to work!
These suggestions create beautiful effects.

Pine Boughs

Feathers

Roots

Weeds

Mix paint to a medium consistency and provide lots of colors.
Abstract pictures in shades of green are lovely too!

Nature Dyes

Beautiful, vibrant dyes or neutral colors can be made from
plants and berries, coffee, tea and fruit juices.
Try these and others that are natural to your area.

**Grass, Dandelions, Strawberries, Blueberries,
Spinach, Flower Petals**

Soak in warm water for a few hours. Bring dyestuff to a boil
and simmer for one hour. Cool and pour through strainer.
Dissolve 4 Tbsp. of alum and 4 Tbsp. of cream of tartar in
1 cup of water. Add to the dye mixture.
Add water to get desired shade.

Now the children can dye wool yarn or bits of
cotton and flannel.

Summer is the perfect time to wander through woods and stroll through meadows enjoying nature at its finest. Children at this age seem to appreciate the little things like lady bugs and dandelions. It's important to provide as many opportunities as possible for being in the great outdoors.

Pet Rock

Have each school-ager create their own "pet rock."
Select rocks that are smooth on top and about three inches in diameter.

Let each child paint their rock with tempera paint. Encourage them to be creative and follow a theme if they would like. After paint has dried, glue eyes in place (these can be made from construction paper, but are most effective when purchased from hobby stores and have moveable eyeballs).

Examples Of Pet Rocks

ZANY ZEBRA: Black and white
JOLLY GIRAFFE: Brown and gold pattern
LAMB: Paint white; cover with cotton
FLASHY FISH: Paint silver; cover with sequins
POKEY PUPPY: Paste on ears; add ribbon for leash
FEATHERED FRIEND: Paint and glue on craft feathers

Pet Rock Homes

Every pet rock needs a suitable home!

BERRY BASKETS FOR ZOO CAGES
BOX WITH GRASS OR HAY FOR LAMB
PLASTIC CEREAL BOWL FOR FISH TANK
BOX FOR DOG HOUSE
EMPTY BIRD NEST OR TREE BRANCH FOR BIRD

Adopt A Tree

Have the school-agers find a tree in a nearby park
or on the playground that they will "adopt."
Help them learn just how important trees are to us.
Set aside special times for taking care of the tree and
help them sharpen their observation skills
by recording changes that occur.

Collect seeds from the tree.
Collect leaves from the tree.
Keep a record of observations.

Some Things For School-agers To Know:

- Nothing can take the place of a tree.
- Trees produce oxygen
  that helps us breathe.
- Trees give us food, paper, lumber
  and lots more.
- Trees provide homes for animals.
- Trees give us beauty and shade.
- A tree can be saved by recycling
  a stack of newspapers three feet high.

Trees Are Valuable To Planet Earth!

Smelly Collage

Give each child a selection of spices
such as cinnamon, parsley, black peppercorns,
nutmeg and cloves.
Provide glue and construction paper.
Not only do these collages smell heavenly
they look great too!

Potato People

Give each child their very own potato.
Provide a selection of noodles, parsley,
yarn, raisins and toothpicks.
Give the potato personality by letting
each child put facial features and hair
on their potato person.
How about making a whole family?

Make a collar for each potato from a
strip of paper taped together in the back.
Insert the potato head so that it can
stand up and be seen as a real personality!

Leaf Rubbing

Some ideas never die because they're so neat.
Make a beautiful nature picture
by rubbing over leaves.
Peel paper from a crayon and
rub it across paper
until it becomes flat on one side.
Lay a thin sheet of paper over
an arrangement of leaves that have
been taped onto a table.
Rub the crayon over the leaves
to see a beautiful picture appear.
Different types of weeds and
flowers also may be used.

Build A Bird Nest

Think like a bird! Go on a walking field trip and collect small twigs,
feathers, bits of paper, string, leaves, etc.
Mix soil and water together to make a thick muddy "paste."
The kids can work on the bird nest as a collective project or
each can build their own. If at all possible, try to have a sample bird nest for
observation. Remind children that it will take a few days, because mud needs
to dry before too many twigs are piled on. This project gives everyone a
new respect for birds as architects!

OUTDOOR GAMES

Summer is the perfect time to get plenty of exercise in the great outdoors. Games that require lots of space like tag and all types of relay races are perfect activities for keeping the body physically fit.

Wagon Wheel Tag

This game is best played on a sandy beach or a flat sandy playground.
Trace a large circle about 12 feet in diameter onto the beach or playground.
Next, put in the spokes.
Whoever is chosen to be the "WAGON MASTER" must tag the players as they run by without stepping off the wagon wheel lines.
The players get as close to the wagon master as they dare, but they cannot step on the spokes or the rim of the wheel.
The last person to be caught becomes the new wagon master.

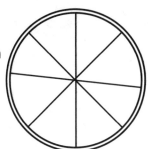

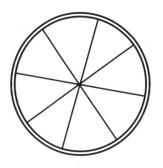

H∞la Hopping

Place Hoola Hoops on the ground in a random pattern and jump in and out of them. Have the children try jumping "rope" with the Hoola Hoop. There aren't too many places to hide a Hoola Hoop, but have them give it a try.

Have a brainstorming session to see who can come up with the best Hoola Hoop game. It's amazing what can be done with a circular tube!

Statue Spin

Choose a person to be "THE SCULPTOR" and
another person to be "THE BUYER."
The sculptor twirls each player around by one arm.
The players, when they quit spinning, must freeze
in the position they land in. Now it's time for the buyer
to choose the very best statue for her art collection.
The statue that is chosen then becomes the "sculptor"
for the next set of spins. The "buyer" chooses a player
to be the next statue buyer.

Hidden Treasures

Before the game begins, hide small bags of
M&M's around the playground.
These become the hidden jewels.

Put a twist on an old treasure hunt game by setting
time limits so that everyone uses their best running skills.

Divide the treasure hunters into two teams and have them
choose a name for their team. Put two empty shoe boxes
in the middle of the play space. These will serve as the treasure chests.

At the word "GO" the players run to find the jewels and
bring them back to their treasure chests. When all the
treasure has been retrieved, count to see which team
found the most.
Have a few jewels for snack!

Stilt Stompers

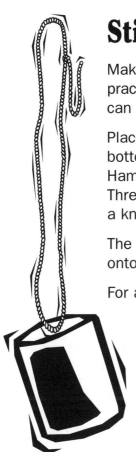

Make some stilts and let the school-agers practice until they're perfect. Hopefully everyone can have their own set!

Place two holes opposite each other near the bottom of a medium sized coffee can. Hammer a nail in the metal to make the holes. Thread a rope through the holes and tie a knot so the rope is about waist-high on each child.

The children put their feet on the can and hold onto the rope as they walk.

For an added challenge, set up an obstacle course!

Mother May I ?

Don't forget this old favorite!

Choose someone to be the "mother" and have the "children" stand behind a marker. The object of the game is to get to the mother first.

The "mother" chooses the kind of step that may be taken, but the "children" must remember to ask "Mother, May I?" before taking a step or they lose a turn.

TYPES OF STEPS:
baby steps, giant steps, scissor steps, tiptoe steps, umbrella steps (make up your own!)

Summon up some school spirit! Choose a day to honor the school or your program. Let the school-agers come up with some of their own ideas. Make sure to have school or program colors, a school or program T-Shirt, maybe even a school or program song!

School COLORS

Ask the school-agers to wear the school or program colors. If there are no official colors, choose some to represent the summer program.

Summer T's

Ask school-agers to bring an old white T-shirt to the summer program. Make sure it is okay to personalize them with school or program colors.

Cut star shapes from sponges. Mix fabric dye according to directions in appropriate colors and pour into shallow styrofoam meat trays. Ask children to dip star shapes in the paint and then print onto their T-shirts.

Put some of the paint in squirt bottles like recycled mustard and hand lotion bottles for personalizing with a name. Ask children to write their names on the shirts with a pencil before squirting paint onto the outline. Wash in COLD water!

Pennant Power

Make a pennant pattern from newspaper or cardboard.
Pin the pattern to a piece of felt and ask the school-agers to trace around it.
After cutting it out, decorate with markers, sequins, puffy paint, etc.
The pennants may be used to decorate the program's main room and later taken home by each child.

Secret Handshake

Create a special handshake for only the summer school-agers to know. Give each child plenty of time to practice the handshake. Make a pact that no one will tell anyone else about the secret handshake, especially the other kids in the after school program in the fall.

Have A "Dress-Up" Day

Decide ahead of time that everyone will wear a certain kind of clothing like dressy clothes or old clothes, or maybe a certain color of clothing.

Mummy Wrap Relay

Crepe paper is cheap and may be used again and again.
Buy a few rolls in school colors.

Divide the kids into two groups.
Tell each team to choose a representative to be their "SPIRIT MUMMY."

Give the two teams equal amounts of crepe paper and at the word "GO," tell them to start wrapping their "SPIRIT MUMMY" as fast as possible.
The crepe paper must be wrapped relatively evenly without large gaps, but not <u>too</u> tight!

Whichever team gets their mummy wrapped first from head to toe is the WINNER!

ADULT SUPERVISION NEEDED TO ENSURE "MUMMY" DOESN'T FALL OVER.

Brainstorming

Have a brainstorming session in which the school-agers think about what they and their friends might do well.

Examples Of Jobs That Might Be Appropriate:

BABYSITTING	WASHING CARS
CLEANING	WEEDING GARDENS
PET CARE	BAKING / COOKING
MOWING LAWNS	CLEANING

Children often find themselves with extra time on their hands during summer months. The best and most profitable remedy may be cashing in by doing odd jobs and chores around the house or even around the neighborhood. At any rate, encouraging school-agers to think about what they do best is a valuable tool in building self-awareness.

Job Concentration

Have each child bring in the employment wanted section of the newspaper. Select about 10 to 15 jobs and clip them out. Cut index cards into fourths. Next, glue the ads onto the cards. Children can play a concentration game with the cards or for younger children, a matching game would be fun.

Yellow Pages Ad

Ask children to look in the Yellow Pages to see what kinds of descriptions are needed to advertise job skills and services. Let them make up their own Yellow Pages ad. Make sure the ads include the following information:

TYPE OF SERVICE OFFERED
NAME OF COMPANY
PHONE NUMBER
TIMES AVAILABLE
SNAPPY SLOGAN OR EYE CATCHING LOGO

Job Collage

Cut the Yellow Pages from old phone books.
Let children cut out the ads and glue
them onto construction paper for a job collage.

Design A Business Card
Or Flyer

Let children design their own business cards or flyers to describe what they do
best. Flyers may be designed on regular typing paper or construction paper.
Print shops will be happy to donate left-over business card stock.
Encourage children to think of a name for their business, a logo,
and a snappy slogan or jingle.

Career Charades

Ask children to act out these jobs and see
who can guess the correct answer first.
*Fire Fighter, Custodian, Cowboy, Mail Carrier,
Doctor, Astronaut, Teacher, Artist, Police Officer*

Non-Traditional Roles

Children enjoy discussing things with adults.
To stimulate discussion, ask questions like:

*"Can men be nurses, flight attendants and secretaries?
Can women be construction workers and truck drivers?"*

Maybe a parent who works in a non-traditional role
can come and speak to the summer program kids.

Barefeet Fun

It's fun to go barefoot in the good old summer time.
Try barefoot painting on a long strip of butcher paper.
Trace around bare feet on a sheet of paper and
turn it into a person with personality. Sit on the floor
and try picking up a tissue with bare feet.
Have school-agers tickle each other's feet with a feather.

Wet Sponge Throw

Set up some empty cans and plastic bottles as targets.
Soak some sponges in water. Have the campers line up
behind a marker and see if they can hit the targets.

It's difficult to
predict where
a wet sponge
will go!

Summer SPLASH ART

Fill some large spray bottles with tempera paint.
*(It must be mixed very thin so that it doesn't clog holes
of spray bottles.)*

Place a large sheet of butcher paper or newspaper
on a fence or hang on a temporary clothesline.
Let two or three children at a time create a group painting.

Watermelon Popsicles

On a hot summer's day, cool down with this refreshing treat! Slice a watermelon into one inch thick slices. Next, cut into rectangle or pie shapes and insert a popsicle stick through the rind. Wrap in plastic wrap and freeze about 3 hours until firm.

Lid Landing

Fill a large tub or wading pool with water. Collect lids from peanut butter and jelly jars and float them on top.

Have school-agers stand behind a starting line and give each of them a few marbles or small pebbles and see if they can throw them into the lids. The starting point may be moved back with each throw to create a bigger challenge.

CAR WASH

Have a car wash. It's fun, it's easy.

School-agers can learn a lot from organizing a car wash right in your parking lot.

THINGS TO DO:

Decide who the customers will be:

Staff, parents, community etc.

Decide on a fair price.

Decide on how the money will be spent.

Make posters and display them around the community.

Collect buckets, sponges, drying cloths, etc.

SPLASH DAY

Have school-agers bring swimsuits,
towels and sunscreen for a
special water day right
on the playground.

**TRY SOME OF
THESE ACTIVITES:**

Fill up water balloons
and toss them
back and forth.

Set up different types
of sprinklers
and run through them.

Make sure plenty of water is near
the sandbox - it makes building more fun!

Create your own water slide by letting
water from the hose run down the slide.

Make a rainbow by standing with your back
to the sun and spraying water into the air.

Put water in cups with a little tempera paint.
Provide old paint brushes for painting on the sidewalk.

Have a wash day and wash everything from
doll clothes to swing sets.

Mix a little tea or coffee in a dishpan with water.
Place paper in the water and
let dry in the sun for a parchment effect.

Summertime is travel time! Encourage school-agers to turn the program into a travel agency.

Decorate the room with travel posters - travel agencies will donate their outdated posters. Collect travel magazines and travel sections from the Sunday papers for use with this theme.

Design A Travel Poster

Ask the school-agers where they would go if they could go anywhere in the whole world. Likely responses will be Hawaii, Paris, etc. Encourage them to seek out places that might not be so well known. Have globes and maps around for them to look at. How about Timbuktu? There really is such a place. It's in Africa. There are many exotic places to visit and many adventures to have!

For this art project, provide large sheets of poster board if possible. Its smooth surface and larger size will look more like an actual poster.

When finished, hang the posters in the room for decoration.

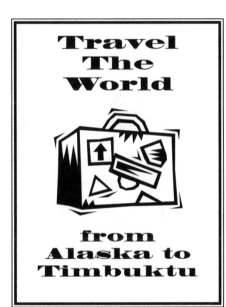

Travel The World

from Alaska to Timbuktu

Packing Riddle

Why couldn't both elephants go swimming at the same time?

They only packed one pair of trunks!

Packing Relay

Fill a suitcase with clothes and some other items like toothbrushes, soap, belts, and shoes. Place an empty suitcase opposite the packed one, about 10 to 12 feet away.

Divide children into two teams. The first two players must run to the packed suitcase, select an item, run back and put it in the empty suitcase before the next person on the team can start.

Whichever team finishes packing the suitcase first is the winner!

Tourist Treats

Serve some foods that are found in other countries.

EXAMPLES:
fresh pineapple, burritos, spaghetti, pita bread, eggrolls, croissants, fortune cookies, rice cakes, etc.

Flag Waving

Countries design different flags to represent their countries. Show pictures of flags and have children make up a country and create a flag for it. Ask them questions like:

Does it snow in your country?
Are you near an ocean?
What type of food do you eat?
What kind of clothes do you wear?

Packing List From A To P

Use the Packing List on page 137.
Copy one for each child or have them number papers from 1 to 16.
Ask them to list things they would take on a trip that begin with the letters:
A B C D E F G H I J K L M N O P

EXAMPLE: alarm clock, bathrobe, chips, diaper

Traveling Games

Traveling can be boring if there's nothing to do.
Pretend to be traveling and play these games.
Make up some games as a group.

Pack A Pickle

Choose someone to be "IT."
That person begins the game
by saying, "I'm going on a trip
and I'm taking a pickle."
The next player adds to
the list by saying,
"I'm going on a trip and
I'm taking a pickle and a kitten."
The person who remembers
the most items without leaving
any out begins the next game.

 # I Spy

Try spying things along the way.
Play this game when going on the next field trip!

Road Signs:

Stop, Yield, Railroad Crossing, Speed Limit, Detour,
One Way, No Passing

Animals: cows, sheep, horses, pigs, dogs

Car Types And Colors: convertibles, station
wagons, jeeps

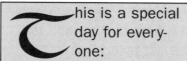

This is a special day for everyone:

THE UN-BIRTHDAY DAY! Celebrate everything exactly opposite than at a birthday party!

Now there's a new reason to party even if you don't have a birthday during the summer months!

UN-BiRTHDAY PARTY

Un-Birthday Attire

Since people usually want to look their best at a birthday party this is not a day for dressing up. Tell the school-agers to wear their oldest clothes to the un-birthday party.

Un-Present Give-Away!

Have each child select and wrap something silly that no one would really want for a present! The presents should be wrapped in plain brown paper from grocery bags or comic newspapers.

Something New For An Un-Present?—NO WAY!

How about these silly ideas?

Rock, Acorn, Wilted Flower, Stale Cookie, Stick, Used Coloring Book, Empty Gum Wrapper

Put on some music, anything but "Happy Birthday!" Ask the school-agers to sit in a circle. Select one of the UN-BIRTHDAY PRESENTS and let children pass it around until the music stops.

Whoever ends up with the UN-BIRTHDAY PRESENT gets to open it.

Un-Birthday Cake

A FROSTED CAKE FOR THE UN-BIRTHDAY?—NO WAY!
How about a CAULIFLOWER CAKE?

Wash a cauliflower and place it in a bowl.
Cut carrots into small two inch strips.
Stick them in between florets on cauliflower.
These are the UNCANDLES of course!

ICE CREAM FOR THE UNBIRTHDAY?—NO WAY!
How about something really nutritious like a creamy vegetable dip?

Mix up a vegetable dip and give each child a spoonful
beside their UN-BIRTHDAY CAKE!

Hide The Candle

MAKE A WISH AND LIGHT THE CANDLES?—NO WAY!
How about not making a wish and hiding the candles?

Play a hide and seek game with real candles.
Select one person to be "IT."
While everyone else closes their eyes,
"IT" hides the candles around the room.
This is a pretty challenging game,
because candles are small and
can get into the smallest places!

20 Questions
Wishing Game

Everyone has things they wish for whether it's their birthday or not. Give each child a chance to think up something they wish for, then let the other children ask 20 questions about the wish. If no one guesses the right wish, the child gets another turn.

EXAMPLE:
Wish: *A Horse*

Question: *Are you wishing for something to eat?*
Answer: *No*
Question: *Is it a toy?*
Answer: *No*
Question: *Is it an animal?*
Answer: *Yes*
Question: *Does it bark?*
Answer: *No*

Un-Birthday
Word Scramble

Use the UN-BIRTHDAY WORD SCRAMBLE on page 145.

WE DO NOT WANT BIRTHDAY WORDS AT OUR UN-BIRTHDAY PARTY so we've scambled the letters.
Try to pronounce the un-birthday words!

DACELN
AKCE
RSTNPEE
AMECR EIC
RSEISRUP
MSGEA
TCINORADEO

Even in the middle of July, school-agers can play cool games, build snowmen and create winter wonderlands.

These icy activities and recipes will definitely COOL everyone down no matter what the weather!

Make A Winter Wonderland

This craft recipe must be closely supervised by an adult.
MIX CRYSTALS OUTSIDE OR IN WELL-VENTILATED ROOM.

Crystal Recipe

6	tbsp. salt
6	tbsp. bluing
6	tbsp. water
1	tbsp. ammonia

Mix the ingredients in a bowl.

To create your winter scene, place artificial trees, mini-houses, plastic animals, etc. in a shallow ceramic bowl or styrofoam meat tray.

You can make little houses from boxes or blocks and trees by placing twigs into thread spools.

When the scene is ready, carefully spoon crystal recipe over the objects. Remember, the crystals are extremely delicate and will shatter if moved. Find a good safe place for your scene and watch the crystals begin to grow in a couple of hours. They will continue to grow for a day or two.

Snowmen

Give each school-ager a sheet of black construction paper and a piece of white chalk. Tell them you want them to draw a snowman. Sounds simple enough, but it's tricky, because they have to put the paper on a table, turn around and draw the snowman without looking!

Snowballs

Have the children make up a batch of these delicious snacks
that will melt in their mouth!

INGREDIENTS

1   cup powdered sugar
2   tbsp. margarine
1 1/2 cup Krispy cereal
1/2   cup chopped nuts
1   cup peanut butter
coconut
powdered sugar

Mix ingredients except powdered sugar and coconut.
Form the mixture into small balls and
roll in powdered sugar and coconut.

SNOWBALL FIGHT

Keep the children busy for a few minutes
crunching newspapers into two inch snowballs.

Divide the children into teams and line them up about 5 feet away from each
other. At the word "GO," let them toss their "snowballs" at each other!

Ice Tossing

Line the children up in two rows exacty
opposite each other with about 3 feet in between.

Give each child in one row an ice cube. They must throw the ice cube to the
person opposite them. Remember the ice cube melts fast! Whichever pair of
children has the ice cube the longest wins the game!

Winter Words

Go to the Winter Wonderland page on page 147.
See how many three and four letter words
the children can find in the words, **WINTER WONDERLAND.**

COLD CHOCOLATE

Instead of serving ice cold lemonade, serve "cold chocolate."
Mix cocoa according to directions for hot chocolate,
place in the refrigerator until chilled and serve with an
ice cube instead of a marshmallow.

Ice Cube Game

Have school-agers sit in a circle. Put on some lively music and
ask children to pass the ice cube behind their backs from one
to the other. The object is to get rid of the ice cube as quickly
as possible so you're not stuck with it when the music stops!

Ice Milk Cones

Flavor milk with vanilla, almond, or
peppermint flavoring.
Freeze in ice cube trays.
After freezing, place in plastic baggies,
crush with a kitchen mallet
(children love this part)
and serve in ice cream cones.

ICE CUBE PAINTING

Mix liquid tempera paint with water
before freezing in ice trays.

Give each child a sheet of
white constructiion paper and
let them paint with the cubes.
These make pretty pastel
water colors. Provide a container
for ice cubes as they melt.

Art experiences for children are a valuable means of self-expression. Children have an abundance of creativity!

At this age, it's important to encourage them to be innovative and experiment freely with colors, textures, and techniques. Remember, it's the PROCESS that's important, not the finished product. Select a few of these projects and keep your school-agers busy for hours!

Dotty Art

This activity is great fun and it isn't even messy!
Provide children with any type of paper for the background.
Give them a selection of signal dots in all sizes and colors.
They are inexpensive because there are hundreds in each
package or on each roll—purchase them at any
office supply store.

Tell children to think of a picture they want to create.
It can be an actual object like a flower or an abstract design.
All they have to do is peel off the dots and stick them
onto their paper.

FingernAil PAinting

Save your fingernail paint brushes, they make excellent art
tools for school-agers. Clean the brush thoroughly with
fingernail polish remover and it's ready for artistic use!
Supply paper and paint and lots of time—
children will do the rest!

Eggshell Mosaic

Boil some eggs for snack and
save the eggshells.
To dye the eggshells,
place them in 3/4 cup of alcohol
mixed with food coloring.
Leave them in the dye until
the desired shade is reached.
Let children create their own
mosaics by glueing the
eggshell pieces onto paper.

Rolling Pin Picture

Put an eye dropper in each shallow container of paint. Tell school-agers to squeeze the paint onto their paper from the droppers in little blobs. Remind children to use one eye dropper for each color of paint.

When this step is finished, cover the picture with another sheet of paper. Let each child roll back and forth with rolling pin over their paintings. Lift off carefully for beautiful results!

Pounce Painting

Mix tempera paint in bright colors and place in meat trays or margarine lids. Give each child a few Q-tips and tell them to dip the swab in the paint and "pounce" (dab) it onto their pictures. These paintings will be treasured!

Burlap Weaving

Cut pieces of colored or natural burlap into twelve inch squares *(the rougher the burlap, the better.)*

Let children create some lovely weavings by unraveling the burlap. They can pull vertical or horizontal threads out. Threads can also be squeezed together in hour glass shapes and tied.

Stitching And Bead Making

Native Americans produce intriguing designs stitched on cloth and leather. The following art activities can develop into extended projects that children take great pride in finishing. It also gives them an opportunity to learn about different cultures.

STITCHING St★rs

Before beginning this next project, read "Quillworker: A Cheyenne Legend" by Terri Cohlene, published by Watermill Press.

This is a delightful legend about a young girl who created beautiful designs from dyed porcupine quills. She stitched warrior suits from buck skin for her seven adopted brothers. Wearing their shimmering starburst designs they eventually became the North Star and the Big Dipper.

After reading the story, let children model designs from the pictures in the book. Older children may stitch with a large darning needle on burlap. Younger children will have success with a bobby pin threaded with yarn and loosely woven burlap.

Bead Necklaces

Many cultures make their own beads for necklaces.
Beads may be made from coffee beans, shells, seeds,
clay and other materials.
Make a necklace of clay beads using this recipe.

2	cups flour
1	cup salt
1/2	cup water
2	tbsp. alum

Mix the flour, salt, and alum in a small bowl.
Gradually add water until the mixture forms soft modeling clay.

Next, roll a small ball of clay into a bead shape and pierce with toothplcks. After about one day, the beads will be dry and ready to paint. Children enjoy making necklaces and bracelets from their original hand-made beads.

JUNK SCULPTURE

Cut tinfoil into small squares. Collect some interesting objects like spools, beads, popsicle sticks, paper clips, paper tubes, twigs, etc.
Cover objects with tinfoil and glue pieces together.

Art Fair

Get the parents involved by having an art fair.
Invite them to the fair where the children's art is exhibited.
Serve punch and popcorn to turn it into a special event.

Need More Display Space?
Cover an appliance box with wallpaper —**Presto!**
You have four mini-walls for art display.
They're collapsible for easy storing and
they make art look really special!

Backwards Day is a day to switch everything around!

Everyday routines are boring to say the least. Add a little SPICE and a lot of laughter to an ordinary day by doing things in an EXTRAORDINARY manner.

CLOTHES

The day before "Backwards Day" remind children to put some article of clothing on backwards or upside down.
T-shirts can be turned around, shoes put on the wrong feet, socks may be worn that don't match etc.
Tell school-agers to use their imagination—
it's always surprising what they'll come up with!

Greetings

As children arrive, say things like, "Good-bye, Ryan" or, "See you tomorrow, Maria."

The Name Game

Try writing children's names backwards on the chalkboard. Say their names and see if everyone can remember the "new names" all day.

Story Time

Begin reading at the back of the book. This little routine is guaranteed to bring lots of giggles. Be very serious as you read as if you can't figure out what is wrong!

Discussion Time

When you gather school-agers together, sit with your back to them for at least a minute or two and talk as if you're speaking directly to them. Write on the chalkboard from the bottom to the top.

Outside Time

Ask children to walk backwards when going to the playground.
Tell them to be very quiet, and not be too active while outside.
(Don't let this go on too long or you'll have some very active children once you're back inside.) When they line up,
make sure it's a horizontal line not a vertical line!

Snack Time

There are lots of things to do backwards at snack time.
Turn the plates and glasses upside down.
Place silverware at top and bottom of the plate or
place it upside down.

Relays

Divide the group into several teams. Have some type of relay race.
Whichever team comes in last will, of course, WIN the game!

Plan an art activity that takes lots of
fine motor coordination like painting or drawing.
Have school-agers do the project
with their NON-DOMINATE hand!
Be sure to display the art work for everyone
to enjoy. Ask children to put their names
on their papers BACKWARDS!

Word Game

It's always a good idea to strengthen academic skills after school or during the summer. This simple spelling game will keep a few words familiar.
Write some simple words on the board that also mean something
when written backwards.

EXAMPLES: Tip   Pit

Top   Pot

Pan   Nap

Balloon Messages

Give each child a small sheet of paper. Ask them to write a message to someone else in the class and place the rolled up paper inside the balloon. Next, blow the balloon up and let each child tap the balloon toward the person it is being "sent" to. Supervise this activity to make sure every school-ager gets a message from someone.

The receiver of the balloon may pop the balloon and find the message inside.

Make beautiful balloon flowers by glueing uninflated balloons onto construction paper in the shape of a flower.

Supply balloons in a variety of colors for the petals. Green balloons represent leaves, and the stems are drawn on the paper.

What child doesn't love balloons? Balloons can turn an ordinary day into a Magic Monday in no time at all!

Instruct children not to play with balloons that are not inflated. They are easily sucked into the mouth and choked on.

BALLOON TOSS

There are special water balloons available for this activity,
but most balloons work quite well.
Place the lip of the balloon over the faucet,
turn water on and fill balloon—tie off end.
Place balloon carefully in a box or dishpan.

Line children up facing each other.
At first, have them stand only two feet apart
as they toss the balloons back and forth.
With each turn, have them step back a few feet.
PREPARE TO GET WET!

Balloon Bust

Blow up the balloons and tie one onto a leg of each school-ager.
See who can break the balloon first by stepping on it,
sitting on it, etc.
Remind children to be expecting some loud BANGS!

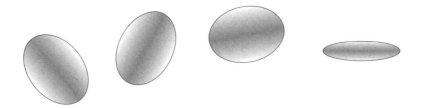

CLOWNING CUT-UP

Let children paint each other's faces. Apply cold cream first for easy take-off later. Face paint can be bought at novelty and magic stores or use the following recipe.

ven the most reserved children like to clown around!

Clown costumes are easy to come up with—the more ridiculous the better!

Face Paint

1/2	tsp. corn starch
1/2	tsp. water
1/2	tsp. cold cream
1	tsp. alum

This paint should be stored in an airtight container. It will stay fresh for several weeks. It may be applied with finger, brushes or Q-tips and it wipes off easily!

Clown Concentration

Reproduce the clowns on page 129. Make several copies. Cut the squares out and glue onto tagboard.

Tell children to turn all of the cards face down. The first player turns two cards over trying to find a match. The next player remembers those cards and turns two more cards over. Each time a match is found, it is placed aside by the player that found it. Whoever finds the most matching sets wins the game.

Pin The NOse On The ClOwn

Use the comic section from the Sunday newspaper for making the clown's clothes. Make the face from construction paper and put yarn sprigs on for hair. Leave the nose off of the face. Use large red signal dots for the nose and give a nose to each player. Put the child's initial on the front.

Tape the clown to the wall. Blindfold each child, spin them around and see if they can get the nose closest to where it really belongs. All they have to do is peel and stick!
USE INDIVIDUAL BLINDFOLDS TO PREVENT TRANSMISSION OF DISEASE.

Paper Plate Clowns

Give school-agers scraps of construction paper, wallpaper, yarn, buttons, feathers, etc. and let them make a clown face on a paper plate.

The rim of another plate may be used for the ruffled collar.
See who can make the funniest clown.

COUPON CLIPPING

Have a coupon day and give coupons for all types of good behavior from cooperating with others to using good manners on field trips.

You may even want to incorporate this as an on-going incentive program and have a COUPON DAY periodically throughout the year. School-agers EARN the coupons and them REDEEM them for special things.

Coupon Pattern

Use the coupon pattern on page 131—make up your own products, services and words of thanks to put on the coupons. Reproduce the page on brightly colored paper.
The new florescent colors are terrific and really make a statement. Laminate the page of coupons front and back with Contact paper before cutting them out.

Sometimes a few minutes of undivided attention with a staff person is the best reward a school-ager can receive!
These coupons can reflect personal awards for special behaviors.

COUPON EXAMPLES:

Reserved board games
Line leader
Washing hands first
Special helper
Program party
Special field trip
Riding in the front seat of van
Small prizes —party favors, pencils, erasers, paper,
     hair barrettes, shoe strings, miniature cars, etc.

A Trip to the Zoo

How To Earn The Coupons:

Children may earn coupons for everything from good behavior
on field trips to extending common courtesies of
"please" and "thank you" to each other.
They may help by assisting with snacks, cleaning up,
repairing board games, sorting out puzzle pieces, etc.
Let children help think of ways to earn the coupons.

EXAMPLES:

Good sports attitude

Excellent field trip behavior

Cleaning the room

Cooperating with others

Good meal-time manners

Quiet rest times

Using "Please" and "Thank you"

Clipping Coupons

Coupons are often clipped from a newspaper
or magazine. Turn coupon clipping into a
fun game and get some cutting practice
in at the same time!

Give each school-ager an old magazine and
a pair of scissors. At the word "Go,"
children turn to the pages with coupons
and clip them out as fast and as neatly
as possible. Set a time limit of three or five minutes.

Coupon Collage

Now that all the coupons are clipped, what can you do with them?
Give children glue and paper and let them make a colorful coupon collage!

Trading Coupons

Let children set up their own bartering system—two popsicle coupons for one
chocolate chips coupon, etc. Or, tell them to pretend they are setting up
housekeeping. They need to find things they can't live without like toothpaste,
laundry detergent, etc.

CRAWLING CRITTERS

Amazing Ant Fact!

Did you know that an ant carrying a leaf or a beetle on its back is the same in weight proportion as a human carrying a hippopotamus?

Ants On A Log

Make a yummy and nutritious snack. Wash and clean celery and cut into three or four inch strips. Spread peanut butter inside and top with a few raisin "ants." Happy crunching!

Feeding Ants

Mix a spoonful of sugar in 1/2 cup of water. With an eyedropper put a few drops of the sugar water around an anthill. Watch what happens!

Sprinkle bread crumbs around an anthill. Watch what happens!

School-agers enjoy watching all types of insects and bugs.

This is a good opportunity to teach them respect for even the smallest creatures.

Spin A Web

Give each school-ager a ten foot long
piece of black yarn. Have the outline
of a spider web laid out on the floor.
Let each child add their yarn to the web.
Does your web look as good as a spider web?

Try again by cutting the yarn into smaller pieces
and gluing the yarn onto paper.
Paint a peanut black and put if in
the corner of the web.

Crawling Caterpillars

Go on a walk and collect tiny twigs.
Give each school-ager some green
or yellow signal dots in small and
medium sizes, some glue and
a sheet of construction paper.

First, have children glue the twigs
onto the paper. Let them dry.
Next, place the dots on the paper
just on top of the twigs.
Finish by giving the caterpillars
some tiny legs, a face and antennae.

Deck Out A Donut

Give each school-ager a plain donut. Supply a variety of toppings and let each child decorate their personal donut anyway they would like. For toppings not so sweet, try chopped nuts, raisins, fresh pineapple and shredded coconut. Ice the donut with peanut butter or cream cheese.

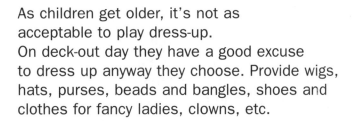

Deck Out Day is short for Decoration Day!

Give the kids a chance to decorate themselves, the door to the program, the playground and a donut. That should keep them busy for awhile!

Deck Out Yourself

As children get older, it's not as acceptable to play dress-up. On deck-out day they have a good excuse to dress up anyway they choose. Provide wigs, hats, purses, beads and bangles, shoes and clothes for fancy ladies, clowns, etc.

After decking out, have a fashion show. Let someone be the narrator as each child parades around the room.

Deck Out The Door

First, cover the door with wrapping paper.
Provide ribbons, tinfoil, spools, beads, feathers (and anything else left over
from arts and crafts projects).
Don't forget the glue.
Children will gladly do the rest!

Deck Out The Fence

If you have a cyclone type fence, this is a great activity.
Give each child some brightly colored crepe paper.
Let them weave it in and out of the fence.
After a few days it will start to disintegrate.
When it does, make sure to remove it
so it doesn't become litter!

DAZZLING DRAMA

nside those school-agers are actors screaming to get out! Props, face make-up, wigs and masks seem to give even the quietest children a lot of confidence.

Vocabulary Building

This is a good opportunity to learn some new words:

props, scripts, stage, curtain call, impromptu, costumes, make-up, drama, comedy, scenes, Broadway

Acting Practice

Make an acting book by cutting interesting character pictures from a magazine, such as clowns, animals, Santa Claus, etc.

Anyone interested in impromptu acting practice may join the troupe. When a picture is shown, the actors must act the part or copy the expression.

Shadow Shifting

Have children divide into pairs and stand facing each other.

When one person moves, the other person *(the shadow)* moves in exactly the same way. Start with the hands and arms and gradually work on facial expressions and more subtle moves.

This takes a lot of concentration and also brings out a lot of laughter!

Script Writing

This is another way to review writing skills in a painless way.
School-agers come up with good plays based on plots
centering around royalty, sunken treasure and desert islands.
Let them write the play down, practice it and act it out!

Kings And *Queens*

Use the crown pattern on page 133.
Give each child a copy. Let school-agers cut out
jewel shapes from tinfoil and colored construction paper.
Add sequins and glitter for a sparkling royal crown of jewels.

For a robe, any large piece of fabric will do, even a sheet.
Necklaces and rings complete the royal costume. Children
are quite good at making up simple scripts to go along
with this theme.

PERKY Pirate

Let school-agers make a pirate hat from black construction paper.
They can decorate the hat with white chalk.

Make a sword and cover it with tinfoil.
Eye patches, gold earrings and bandannas
complete this costume.

DESIGN A BANDANNA: Cut an old white sheet into twelve inch squares.
Supply school-agers with fabric and fabric markers and let them design their
own bandannas to wear around their heads or legs.

Mini Gardens

Give each child the bottom half of an egg carton, a spoon, and some soil mix. Spread newspapers on a table and let each child fill their egg cartons with dirt.

Next, give them a variety of seeds such as marigolds, beans, grass, and lettuce. Ask them to plant one or two seeds in each section. Every day they can water the seeds and watch them grow. For a neat science activity, record what type of seed is planted, when it germinates, etc.

Flower Art

Weeds are beautiful! You may need to check for allergies before planning this activity. Go on a walking field trip and let children select wildflowers and weeds. Back at the classroom, children can remove petals, stems and leaves and recreate the flowers into a three dimensional picture on construction paper.

Seed Snacks

Have a discussion about seeds and how we eat them. For snacktime, serve peanuts, and sunflower seeds. Even popcorn is a seed. What about coconut? Yes, that's a seed too! They're yummy and so nutritious!

Seed Collage

Art using seeds is a very creative experience.
Supply a variety of seeds that vary in size, shape and color.
EXAMPLES: beans and peas, popcorn, sunflower seeds and peanuts.

Let children create beautiful pictures by gluing the seeds on the paper in abstract designs, smiley faces, sailboats, flowers, etc.,

CRYSTAL GARDENS

If it's too cold to go outside, it's the perfect time to grow a crystal garden inside! With just a few ingredients, school-agers can grow their own shimmering crystals in baby food jars.

First, place a sponge, piece of charcoal or crunched up paper towel in the bottom of the baby food jar.

Next, mix the solution for crystals:

6	tbsp. salt
6	tbsp. liquid bluing
6	tbsp. water
1	tbsp. household ammonia

Put a few teaspoons of the mixture into the baby food jars.
If colors are desired, place a drop or two into the jar.
Crystals begin to grow in about an hour.

Three things to remember: **1)** CONTAINER FOR CRYSTALS SHOULD BE CERAMIC OR GLASS, NOT FOIL OR METAL. **2)** MIX CRYSTALS IN A WELL VENTILATED ROOM. **3)** MAKE SURE THIS ACTIVITY IS WELL SUPERVISED!

Celery Sipping

Water travels up the roots and through the stems of plants.
Try this experiment to show how plants take a drink.
Place toothpicks on either side of a stalk of celery. Put some
red food coloring in a glass filled with water. Put some
blue coloring in another glass filled with water.
Put a stalk of celery in each glass balancing the toothpicks
on the rim of the glass to keep the celery from sinking.
Ask school-agers what they think will happen. *Wait and see!*

Spongy Seeds

Dampen a sponge and place it on a saucer. Plant grass seed
in the crevices of the sponge. Keep it moist at all times and
place it in a sunny window. "Mow" the grass with scissors
when it needs clipping!

Soil Samples

Set up an interesting science center by asking each child to
bring a sample of soil found in their yards. They can place
the soil in plastic baggies or put them in bowls for comparing.

Compare the colors and textures.
Is the soil black or brown, fine or coarse?

For even more fun, take a closer look with a magnifying glass.

Make this a lucky day for school-agers!

Make it a Magic Monday by changing the rules a little, having a treasure hunt, and in general jazzing up the day!

Lucky Letters

Before children arrive, tape letters under the chairs used during snack.

Place corresponding letters in a bowl. When all the children are seated for snack, choose a random letter from the bowl. Whoever is sitting in the "LUCKY" seat is the winner. Have a few small prizes on hand for this activity.

A D B X M G K

Bubble Gum Chew

Sometimes children aren't allowed to chew gum in a school-age program, but today is different because it's a lucky day!

Tell children, "This is your lucky day," as you pass out the sugarless bubble gum. Really surprise them by passing out another piece, and another. Now, have a contest to see who can blow the biggest bubble!

Who Is The Luckiest In The Class?

Have some lively discussions by asking simple questions like:

Do you ever feel lucky?
What's a Leprechaun?
Is there a pot of gold at the end of the rainbow?

Discuss lucky symbols like four leaf clovers,
a rabbit's foot, horse shoes, etc.

Treasure Hunt

A treasure hunt is so easy to organize and so much fun for children!
Hide small bags of cereal mixed with M&M's around the room
before school-agers arrive. At the word, "GO,"
school-agers begin their search for the
hidden treasure. Make sure every child
finds at least one bag of goodies.

Mother's Day Tea

Plan a Mother's Day Tea at the end of class on Friday. Children enjoy celebrations and this is a great way to help them honor our traditional Mother's Day.

Delightful Decorations

Decorate a paper tablecloth with sponge painted hearts. To define each place setting, glue rickrack in a heart shape directy onto the tablecloth.

Heart Tree Centerpiece

Make a heart tree for the centerpiece. Find a nicely shaped tree branch and spray it white. Place it in a flower pot filled with sand. Next, cover the pot with tissue or silver foil. Put the branch in the pot and hang construction paper hearts from the branches.

Tea and Cookies

Cookie Creams: Mix a few drops of food coloring with softened cream cheese. Spread between two wafer cookies.

Serve hot herbal tea in a variety of flavors along with ice cold punch.

others deserve special attention on their special day. Inviting mothers in for refreshments or even for a special program is a great way of involving parents in your program, and the simple gifts are sure to please!

Presents For Moms

Recipe Holder

This is sure to be a useful gift for Mom!
Place Plaster of Paris in the bottom of a
hair spray lid. Before the plaster sets,
stick a plastic fork, tines end up in
the plaster. Thread a recipe card
through the tines of the fork
to keep it clean and easy to read.

To make this present special, copy and glue the "Batch of Love" recipe
onto a card and display it in the holder.

Batch of Love

*Measure out a kiss or two
Stir in a warm bear hug*

*Throw in a little tenderness
And an ounce or two of care*

*Mix together with patience
And don't forget the smiles*

*Mothers have a way
Of showing lots of love.*

Soap Balls

1/2 cup water
4   cups soap flakes
small amount of dry tempera paint
vanilla, peppermint, lemon or almond flavoring

Mix water and a few drops of coloring
in a large bowl. For aroma, put in a drop
of peppermint flavoring for green soap balls,
lemon for yellow, etc. Add the soap flakes
and blend with hands until stiff.
Shape into 1 inch soap balls,
and place in a tiny basket or box.

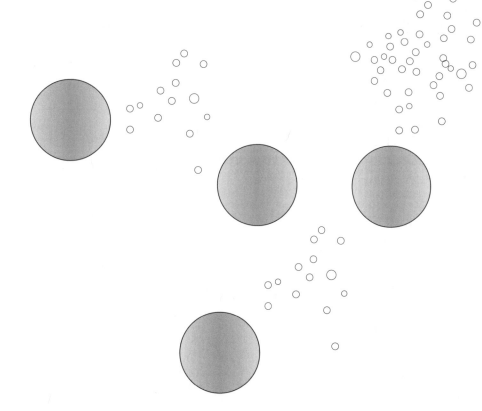

POTPOURRI

cinnamon sticks
crushed flower petals, cedar shavings
(commercial potpourri may also be used)
6 inch fabric squares

Place a spoonful of potpourri
in the center of a fabric square.
Gather edges of fabric
together and tie with
a silk ribbon.

Children love to cook —especially if they get to eat what they cook!

Let school-agers try a few of these recipes.

They can even share with their parents at the end of the day!

Biscuit Bites

1   pkg. refrigerated biscuits
1   small jar apple butter
Cinnamon

Separate biscuits into halves. Spread one of the biscuit halves with apple butter, sprinkle with cinnamon and place the other half on top. Bake as directed. When these are finished, they taste like mini-cinnamon rolls!

Yogurt Sundae Squares

frozen yogurt

sliced bananas

sliced strawberries

chocolate sprinkles

Spread a layer of frozen yogurt in the bottom of an ice cube tray. Place sliced bananas and strawberries over the yogurt.

Top with another layer of frozen yogurt.
Sprinkle with chocolate, and refreeze.
When frozen, cut into squares for a scrumptious dessert!

Creamy Home-made Butter

Make some home-made butter—
it's as easy as one, two, three, or shake, shake, shake!

Pour whipping cream into a baby food jar—1/2 full.
Shake for at least five minutes. Pour off liquid as it separates.
Salt lightly and give each school-ager a popsicle stick
to "churn" the butter with.

Serve on crackers for an unbeatable snack!

Frozen Pudding-Grahams

1 1/2 cups cold milk
1/2   cup chunky peanut butter
1 pkg. *(4 serving)* instant chocolate pudding
24   graham crackers

Blend peanut butter and milk in a bowl. Add pudding mix and beat on lowest speed for about two minutes. Let pudding stand for about five minutes.

Spread filling about 1/2 inch thick on twelve crackers.
Top with remaining crackers, pressing lightly and
smoothing sides with a spatula.
Freeze for about three hours.
Makes one dozen.

Create A New Snack

We're creatures of habit when it comes to eating and most children like to stick to what is familiar to them. But diversity is good and children can be encouraged to try ethnic foods or try putting food together in a different way.

Ask the children in your program about their favorite foods.
One child may like bananas on bagels, another pickles on pita bread.
The important thing is to try something different.

Design A Donut

Buy plain donuts at the store. Give school-agers
a selection of raisins, chopped nuts, coconut,
and sesame seeds.

First, they spread the donut with softened cream cheese—
make colors using a few drops of food coloring.
Next, they decorate. Use decorated donuts in the game below.

Donut Walk

Cut a three inch circle out of the middle of paper plates.
Decorate the plates to look like donuts and place a number on
each plate. Put numbers on the "donut holes" cut from centers
of plates and place in a bowl or basket.

Tape the "donuts" in a large
circle on the floor and put
on some lively music.
Instruct children to
march around the
"donuts" until the
music stops. When it
stops, they stand on
the nearest "donut."
The caller then selects a
"donut hole" from the bowl
and calls out the winning number!

Winner gets to choose a decorated donut to eat
(see activity above)!

have a party full of pizzazz!

You don't have to wait for a holiday to have a celebration complete with special decorations, plenty of food and lots of games. Planning the party is half the fun, so get school-agers involved in making party announcements or invitations.

Balloon Invitations

Balloons are always special and fun to receive. A day or two before the party, give each child a balloon with an invitation tied to the string. An index card works well with a hole punched in one end. Give one to each child as they leave for the day. Be sure to include the date of the party, plus any instructions parents need to be aware of.

Hanging Decorations

These are simple, no mess decorations that turn drab rooms into decorated rooms in a hurry! Bend coat hangers into different shapes. Next, cover them with tinfoil.
Tie ribbons, crepe paper, strings of beads, streamers, etc. onto the hangers and hang them around the room.

Make Your Own Tablecloth

Place a large sheet of butcher paper on the table; tape it under each end to prevent sliding.

Give each child some scraps of colored and print Contact paper. Ask them to cut out different designs like boats, flowers, suns, trees, hearts, balloons, confetti, etc. Next, they get to peel and stick their designs on the tablecloth.
Decorate matching paper plates, napkins and cups too!

Party Poke Cake

What's a party without cake?
This is an easy recipe for children to mix and bake!

1 1/3 cup flour	1 tbsp. vinegar
1 cup sugar	1 tbsp. vanilla
3 tbsp. cocoa	1 cup cold water
1 tsp. soda	powdered sugar
1/2 tsp. salt	
6 tbsp. oil	

Measure dry ingredients into a sifter and sift into a nine inch baking pan.
Poke three holes, spaced evenly into the dry ingredients. Pour oil into the
first hole, vinegar into the second and vanilla into the third. Now, pour cold
water over all. Stir with a fork until blended. Bake for one hour at 375 degrees.
Place the powdered sugar into sifter and sift sugar over the warm cake.
DELICIOUS!

Learning About Celebrations and Ethnic Holidays

People all over the world celebrate holidays important to their culture.
Many celebrations include favorite foods, music, playing games, gift giving
and dancing.

Give the children in your class a chance to tell about their special days.
Read books about Kwanzaa, Chinese New Year, Mardi Gras, Cinco De Mayo,
Hanukkah and other celebrations that might not be familiar to all children.
A great list of holidays is included in *Roots and Wings*, written by Stacey York
and published by Redleaf Press.

Create A Holiday

To emphasize the similarities in celebrations, ask children what kind of holiday
they would like to create. Would it be a holiday honoring a time of year,
a special person, an animal, a happy time in their life?

Let children think of a name for their holiday. Next, they can develop games,
write songs, think of special foods, design costumes and make up dances
for celebrating the special day.

Jello Eating Contest

The day before the party, let school-agers make up a batch or two of Jello.

Place a spoonful of Jello on two paper plates and put the plates on a table. Choose two children to be "it" and start the game.

The object of the game is to eat all the Jello without using hands or eating utensils at all. At the word "Go" children see how fast they can eat the slippery Jello. This is obviously a delightfully messy activity! Have school-agers wear an old shirt and make sure wet paper towels are close at hand!

Feed The Party Animal

Choose someone to be "it." Tell school-agers this must be someone who likes to eat ice cream. This announcement will undoubtedly produce many volunteers! Tie a bib around the "party animal's" neck and seat them in a chair.

Choose another person to be the ice cream feeder. The object is to feed ice cream to the "party animal." The tricky part is that the feeder is blindfolded so, of course, ice cream gets a little out of hand, and out of mouth!
USE INDIVIDUAL BLINDFOLDS TO PREVENT TRANSMISSION OF DISEASE

This game furnishes lots of laughs. Try to give everyone a chance to be the "party animal" or the feeder.
USE PLASTIC SPOONS TO PREVENT DENTAL INJURY.

Walking On Eggshells

When children play this game, they think they are trying to dodge walking on eggs and getting very gooey shoes. Actually, when they hear what they think is the cracking of eggshells, it's really just a pile of crispy cereal!

Show school-agers the eggs scattered in a random pattern on the playground. Tell them they will be blindfolded as they try to pick their way through the maze of eggs without stepping on them and making a real mess!

Have all the school-agers turn their heads or go into another room until it is their turn to be "it." Blindfold the first child, spin them around and let them begin walking. In the meantime, replace the eggs quickly with bags of crispy cereal.

When blindfolded children think they have stepped on an egg, their reactions are very comical! As each child completes the task, they become part of the audience watching the others tiptoe through the eggs.

puzzles present a challenge or a problem that needs to be solved! School-agers enjoy sharing puzzles with their friends and solving puzzles of their own.

Puzzles And More Puzzles

Introduce school-agers to all types of puzzles:

Jigsaw, Crossword, Riddles, Word Searches, Hidden Pictures

Sharing Puzzles

Let children whose names begin with A through E bring a puzzle to the program one day. Continue through the alphabet until everyone has had a chance to participate. This is a great way to introduce new types of puzzles to school-agers.

Fantastic Word Search

Write the words, FANTASTIC SCHOOL-AGERS on the board. See how many words children can think of that can be spelled just by using those selected letters!

Fantastic School-Agers

Personal Puzzle

Have each school-ager cut out a favorite picture from a magazine.
Next, glue it onto a piece of tagboard or a manila file folder.
After it drys thoroughly, divide it into puzzle sections with a pencil and carefully cut along the lines. The puzzles may be stored in baggies and used again.

Word Search

Let each child make their own word search puzzle. **Here's how to do it.**

For a small word search puzzle, line up five letters in a row and make about five or six rows of letters. Make every third letter a vowel and all the rest of the letters consonants.

Next, see how many words can be spelled. The letters have to be next to each other, but they can go up, down or diagonally.

For more word search fun see page 143.

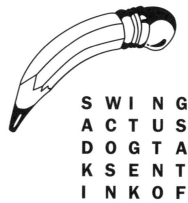

```
S  W  I  N  G
A  C  T  U  S
D  O  G  T  A
K  S  E  N  T
I  N  K  O  F
```

RECYCLE DAY

1 involve the school-agers in some activity that will help the environment.

Children take this topic seriously and this is a chance for them to show they care about what happens to their planet!

FACTS TO KNOW

☞ Recycling means reusing things instead of throwing them in the trash.

☞ 50% of all solid waste has the potential to be recycled.

☞ The paper for one issue of The New York Times takes 62,860 trees.

☞ You can save a tree by recycling a stack of newspapers 3 feet high.

☞ Today, about 10% of our trash is recycled.

☞ Trash is put into landfills and landfills are filling up.

☞ Paper is recycled more than other types of trash.

☞ Trash is made up of: 41% paper, 18% yard waste, 9% metals, 8% food waste, 7% plastics, and 9% other.

THIS SYMBOL MEANS A PRODUCT
WAS MADE FROM MATERIALS
THAT CAN BE

Recycle Poster

Reproduce the symbols on page 139.
Make a poster or book by cutting pictures out of a
magazine or catalogue. Cut out the symbol and
glue it next to everything that can be recycled like
paper, cardboard, newspaper, blueprint paper,
computer paper, wallpaper, etc.

Ten Most Wanted Sign

Use the pattern on page 141.
Give each child a copy to design any way they would like.

Write some of the items on the board that you would like to recycle.
Let children copy the list on to their WANTED: USED AND REUSEABLES sign.
Children may take the sign home and get the whole family involved
in this activity.

After the items have been collected,
take a field trip to a place
that recycles the materials.

Choose Some Of These Things To Recycle:

Newspapers

Aluminum cans

Glass bottles and jars

Plastic containers

Aluminum foil

Computer printout paper

Plastic milk cartons

Cardboard

Paper grocery bags

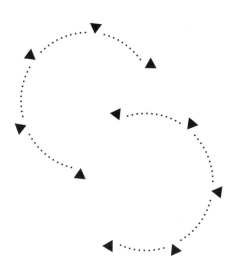

Litter Bags

Recycle grocery bags into official litter collectors.
Make the shoulder strap by folding a sheet of newspaper into a two inch strip. Cut about ten inches off the top of a grocery bag. Staple the newspaper strap onto each side of the bag. Each child needs a bag for collecting litter.

Go on a walking field trip to a local park. See how much litter can be collected from a small area! It's amazing! This activity makes everyone more aware of the problem and what individuals can do!

Music puts magic into Record Day! Give school-agers a chance to share their favorite music by setting aside a day to enjoy all sorts of musical activities.

ROCKIN' RECORD DAY

Bring Your Own

Ask school-agers to bring their favorite record or tape to share with the class. If someone plays a musical instrument, this is an ideal time for them to "perform" for the rest of the class.

Disc Jockey For A Day

Listen to a popular radio station for a few minutes. How does the disc jockey sound? Let children show their own personal talent by being a disc jockey for a day!

Make microphones from paper towel tubes and a ball of tinfoil. Between musical selections, ask for a volunteer D.J. to introduce the song.

DANCING TO THE MUSIC

Have a 50's dance. Make up a new dance!

Make A Hit Single

Have a tape recorder handy for this activity.
Help children make up a class song.

Try using the tune to
"It's A Small World After All".
It will go some thing like this:
"We're a Great Class, After All!"

The sillier the words the more fun!

Song Titles

Give each child a piece of paper and ask them
to make up a title to a new hit song.
Time this activity and give a small prize for the best title.
Let school-agers decide what the winning tune is.

Record Spin

Punch a hole in the middle of a paper plate with a pencil and give one to each school-ager. Put the plate on a record player, turn it on and let children dribble paint on as the record spins. These make great works of art to hang in the room on "Record Day."

Painting To Music

Put on some popular music.
Hang newspaper or large sheets of butcher paper on a fence.
Give children real paint brushes and spray bottles full of
tempera paint. Let them create a musical masterpiece!

Tongue Twisters

Practice saying these over and over, faster and faster!

WALLY WROTE WILD, RECKLESS WORDS

SARA SANG SAD, SIMPLE SONGS

Set aside a special day for sports and physical activities.

Competition is a very real part of our lives, but it's important to emphasize sportsmanship and attitudes. On-going "pep talks" about giving 100% and doing the best possible job give all children a sense of accomplishment even if they don't "win." Awards may be given for best attitude, most spirit, most improved and best effort.

Team T-Shirts

Ask the kids to bring in an old white or
light colored T-shirt.

You will also need fabric dye,
cardboard, pencil erasers and
sponges cut into interesting shapes.

Place a piece of cardboard under
T-shirt material to be stamped.
Practice dipping the pencil eraser or
sponge into dye, pressing it on paper
and lifting it straight up.
Next, decide on a design and
stamp it onto the T-shirt.

After stamping the T-shirts, let them dry.
Colors will not wash out if the T-shirt
is placed in the dryer for 10 minutes.

Stretching

It's always a good idea to warm up before doing
physical activities. Choose a leader and do some
stretching exercises together.

Rope Jumping

Stretch a rope between two children.
Have the other school-agers make a line and
begin jumping over the rope. With each turn the rope
should be lifted off the ground about one inch
until it becomes a hurdle that has to be jumped over.

Make sure the rope is given some slack
as it is moved upward to avoid children falling.

Jump Rope

Make up chants to jump rope by—

Example:

Rita, Rita, jump so high
You can jump and touch the sky
Rita, Rita, jump so low
You can jump very, very slow

Jensen, Jensen, turn around
Now reach down and touch the ground
Jensen, Jensen, jump real fast
See how long you can last!

Team Sports

Depending on the space and equipment available,
play some team sports like basketball, soccer, softball, volleyball

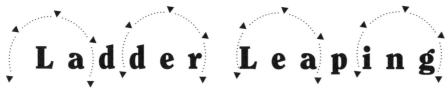

Ladder Leaping

Lay a ladder on the ground. Let children make up some games to play as they leap into and out of the ladder rungs.

DESIGN A RIBBON

Copy the ribbon award patterns on page 149.

Give each school-ager a ribbon and let them design it exactly as they would like. Laminate the ribbon with clear Contact paper for durability.

Track And Relay Races

Take a field trip to a schoolyard
or park that has a track. Let the
school-agers practice endurance runs
as well as short distance sprints.

Position children at different intervals
on the track and let them practice handing
off to each other in a relay race.
Use a paper towel tube for handing off.

Balancing

Get out the balance beam and practice
walking backwards, sideways, barefoot, etc.

Tire Treading

Old tires are just waiting to be recycled.
If you bring them onto your playground,
children will find 101 uses for them.

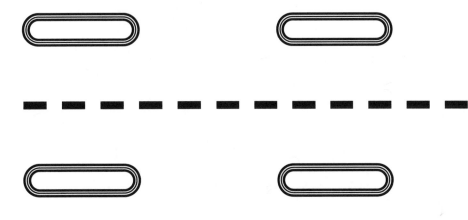

Opening up the old workbench can put magic in any day!

Some of the old-fashioned hobbies are lots of fun for today's children. When children work with tools, close supervision by an adult is needed.

Regular size tools work best for school-agers. This is a great time to teach some safety rules also.

Safety First

Identify tools and demonstrate how to safely use them before letting children work with them.

Nail Pounding

Let school-agers practice pounding nails into something soft like styrofoam and some type of soft wood like pine or fir. Certain types of hard wood like oak and walnut are too difficult for young children to work with. They are usually surprised at what a challenge it is to pound a nail into a board and often have to work at it for quite awhile. But the effort seems to be worth it for the end result!

Sanding

Show children how to sand wood with sandpaper until it is smooth.

Blueprints

Architects throw away tons of blueprints—
you should have no trouble finding lots of donations.
School-agers love to look at the drawings
and fill in the construction lines with markers.
The paper can also be turned over and
used for woodworking drawings on the other side.

Sandpaper Pictures

Give each child a piece of sandpaper and crayons in lots of colors.
After they have created their pictures, glue or staple them onto
a contrasting color of construction paper.

For added interest, the sandpaper may be
cut into geometric shapes, flowers, hearts, etc.

Sawdust Paintings

After you have collected sawdust from your own woodworking projects or from a building site or lumberyard, you will need to color it.

AN ADULT NEEDS TO SUPERVISE THIS ACTIVITY!

Be careful not to inhale the sawdust as you work! Put sawdust in a small bowl. Stir the sawdust with a paint brush that has been dipped in tempera paint. Spread the sawdust on newspaper to dry. You may want to leave some of the sawdust uncolored.

Tell children to think of a design they would like to create and then spread glue on paper. Sprinkle sawdust onto glue (this is like sand painting.) The results are very special!

Wood Collage

Collect wood scraps in all sizes and shapes.
Be sure to include toothpicks, popsicle sticks,
dowel pieces and pegs. A wood base works best
for this project, but if that is not possible,
use a shoe box lid.

Supply plenty of glue and lots of time for these creations.
Some school-agers are sure to be budding architects!

GEOMETRIC BOARDS

This is an easy, mistake-proof project that will provide
a challenge but is not too frustrating!

Most lumber yards are more than happy to donate wood scraps
to centers. The best material for the base of a geometric board
is a nine or twelve inch square of wood about one inch thick.

Give children a piece of wood and a few nails. They can pound
the nails into any pattern they would like. After the nails are in,
rubber bands can be stretched from one nail to another creating interesting designs. Colored rubber bands work best.

Collecting Compliments

Reproduce pages 149 and 151 with the ribbons and "Winner" Words and phrases on brightly-colored paper. Give them out in abundance to the school-agers as you notice their good behavior.

YOU'RE A WINNER!

Small Talk

By now you will have learned special things about each child in your program. Set aside a time to tell each one individually how they are unique. Think of a time they made you laugh, or made you think or made you proud.

1 t's magic when a day is set aside to make everyone feel like a winner.

A little encouragement can go a long way in promoting warm feelings and upbeat attitudes.

Reading

Share a very special book with the kids.
Personalize it by using the children's names
or mentioning them in some way as you read.

Ice Cream Social

Give your children a very special treat.
Have an ICE CREAM SOCIAL.

Besides different flavors of ice cream or
frozen yogurt have plenty of toppings available.
Let each child make their own sundae.

Toppings: raisins, chopped nuts, bananas,
strawberries, coconut, chocolate chips, etc.

Bottle Art from Page 9

Clowns from Page 79

Coupons from Page 19 & 81

Crown from Page 88

Cut two for each child.
Staple crowns together and adjust to fit.

133

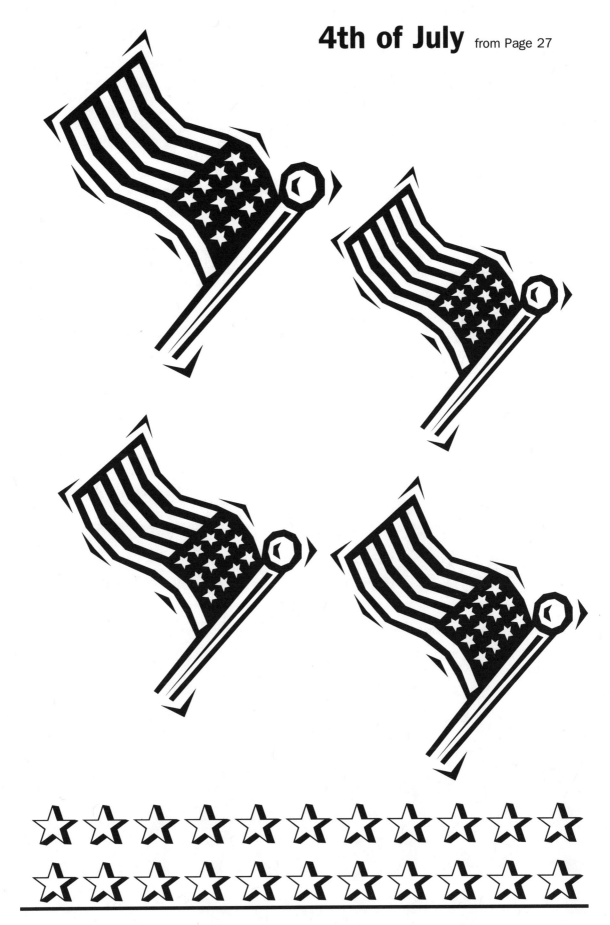

PACKING LIST

Make Your Own Packing List.

List the things you would take on a trip that begin with the letters:

A B C D E F G H I J K L M N O P

Example: An alarm clock, bath robe, chips, diaper

from Page 58

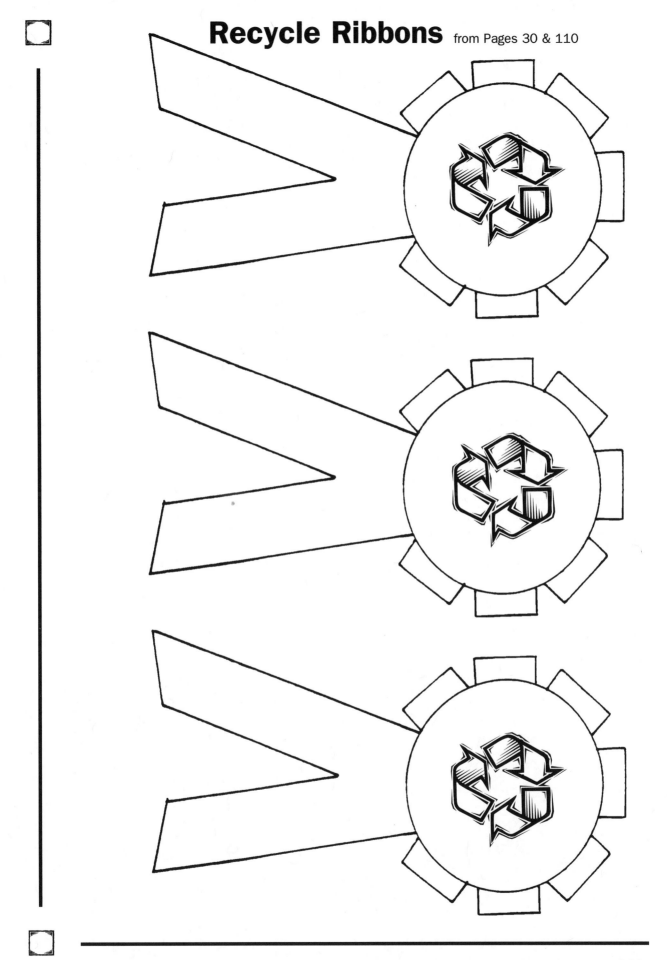

Recycle Ribbons from Pages 30 & 110

WANTED

ITEMS TO RECYCLE
BY SCHOOL-AGERS

from Pages 29 & 110

Spy The Mystery Word from Page 39 & 108

```
I  L  J  G  T  U  D  X  W  P  G
G  N  F  U  G  B  M  S  P  Y  H
S  Q  V  N  R  S  V  E  L  O  Z
A  W  K  E  Y  N  X  C  U  M  A
R  J  M  Y  S  T  E  R  Y  P  D
Q  X  A  F  H  T  G  E  L  O  L
S  K  G  T  B  R  I  T  D  W  G
F  N  I  A  K  T  R  G  E  K  V
S  J  C  L  U  E  S  F  A  Y  A
S  F  H  K  E  Y  I  P  S  T  D
G  R  W  N  G  U  Z  C  O  D  E
```

Un-Birthday Word Scramble

See if you can unscramble these un-birthday "words" to spell birthday words.

Example: Cake, Present, Candle, Ice Cream, Surprise, Decoration, Games

DACELN   – – – – – –

AKCE   – – – –

RSTNPEE   – – – – – – –

AMECR EIC   – – – – – – – –

RSEISRUP   – – – – – – – –

MSGEA   – – – – –

TCINORADEO   – – – – – – – – – –

from Page 63

Winter Wonderland

How many three and four letter words
can you make from the words,
WINTER WONDERLAND?

_____

_____

_____

_____

_____

_____

_____

_____

_____

_____

_____

_____

from Page 66

You're A Winner! from Pages 118 & 125

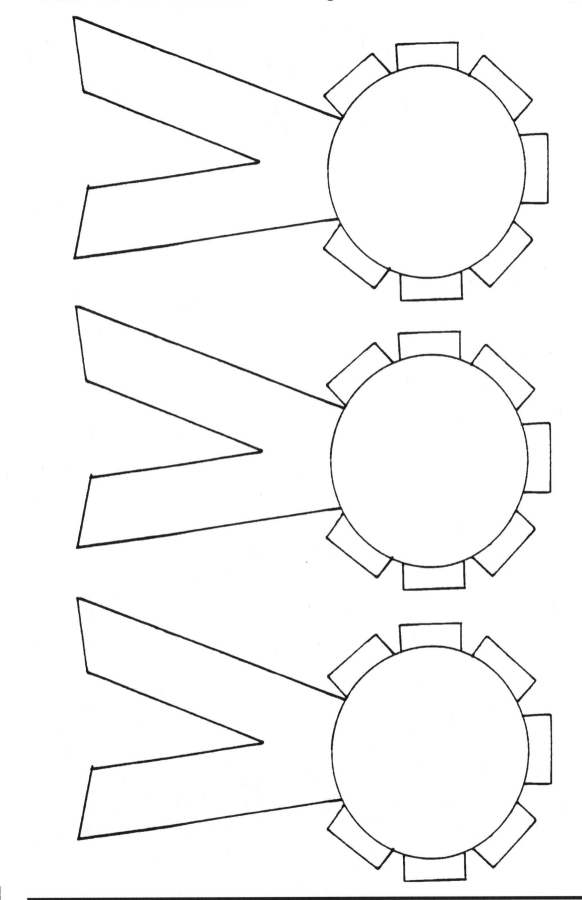

You're A Winner!

149

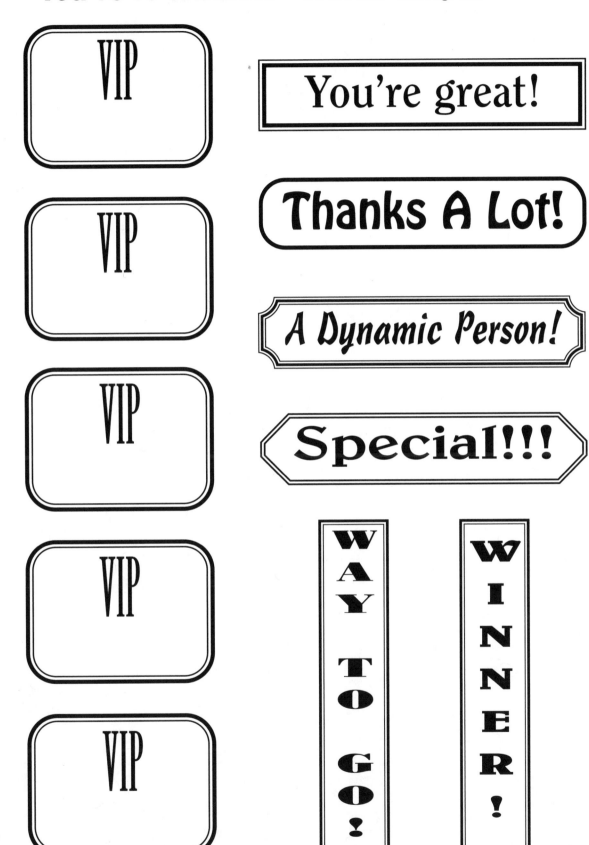

VIP

VIP

VIP

VIP

VIP

You're great!

Thanks A Lot!

A Dynamic Person!

Special!!!

WAY TO GO!

WINNER!